SPECTACULAR RESTAURANTS
of Texas

An Exclusive Showcase of Texas' Finest Restaurants

by Jolie Carpenter

This book is dedicated to my mother, Jonnie Shea, who shares
my love of food and wine. Thanks for being a great cook and
teaching me how food brings people together.

Published by

13747 Montfort Drive, Suite 100
Dallas, Texas 75240
972-661-9884 phone
972-661-2743 fax
www.spgsite.com

Publisher: Brian G. Carabet

Printed in Malaysia

Distributed by Gibbs Smith, Publisher
800-748-5439

PUBLISHER'S DATA

Spectacular Restaurants of Texas

Library of Congress Control Number: 2005934799

ISBN Number: 0-9745747-9-1

First Printing 2006

10 9 8 7 6 5 4 3 2 1

Previous Page: Nick and Sam's, Dallas, Texas
See page 131 Photo by Kevin Marple Hunter
This Page & Facing Page:
Photos by Rick Hunter, Ka Yeung, Michael Wilson
Foreword Page: Del Frisco's Dallas, Texas
See page 63 Photos courtesy of Del Frisco's Dallas, Texas
Introduction Page:
Photo by Danny Piassick
Contents Page:
Photos by Danny Piassick, Terri Glanger, Vernon Wentz

Foreword

Jolie Carpenter has captured the grand elegance and high-style of Texas in her best sellers *Dream Homes of Texas* and *Spectacular Homes of Texas*. This time, with *Spectacular Restaurants of Texas*, she showcases that the Texas restaurant scene is as diverse and divine as it comes.

Spectacular Restaurants of Texas shows the world what Jolie already knows—Texas restaurants rival those of anywhere in the country. From her extensive travels and her lifelong passion for food, wine and interior design, Jolie has selected an impressive collection of the finest culinary gems of Texas. You will get a first-class tour inside some of the most glamorous restaurants of Texas, and you'll meet super star chefs and learn what stirs their creativity.

I respect Jolie because she, like me, is a person who is living the American Dream. She has earned her success through hard work, tenacity and an appreciation for the finer things in life. Her eye for style and culinary passion are revealed in each page of stunning lush photography.

With our Southern hospitality and my favorite motto, "Life is for Living," we invite you to experience the greatest of Texas culinary styles from the classic cuisine of great Texas steakhouses to the thrilling, eclectic, cutting-edge delights of Asian fusion to the international influence of French bistros–it doesn't get bigger or better than Texas.

Bon Appétit!

Dee Lincoln

Dee Lincoln
Del Frisco's Double Eagle Steakhouse

Eating out is a big part of the good life in Texas—especially because Texas restaurants are some of the best in the world. And that is not just my opinion: *Gourmet* magazine, *Food & Wine*, *Travel + Leisure*, *Texas Monthly* and The James Beard House have all given countless awards and high ratings to Texas restaurants and chefs. Just in case you didn't know, Texas has a *first-class* dining scene—this is the reason I've produce Spectacular Restaurants of Texas. The restaurants I have chosen to share with you radiate the style, service and quality cuisine that make for a truly spectacular dining experience.

While researching and writing this book, I met practically everyone in the restaurant business in Texas. I talked to chefs and restaurateurs all over the state, and they all told me the same thing: A stellar dining experience comprises not just high-quality food prepared in fresh, inventive ways; it also requires interior design that moves us, attentive service, and an atmosphere that's warm, comfortable, and conducive to the occasion. They also told me that one of the best things about their jobs is being a part of the celebrations and milestone events in their guests' lives. They all genuinely care about their customers, and that's why they are successful.

I have been lucky enough in both my career and personal life to experience some pretty spectacular dining, from Michelin Guide-rated restaurants in the Burgundy region of France to a sparkling seaside table in Monte Carlo with a breathtaking view of the Mediterranean Sea. Food brings us together for many reasons and the memories that surround these occasions are engrained in us forever. It's not always about the food, for me, it's usually about the friends and family that make a dining experience wonderful.

I have carefully chosen each of these restaurants as the places one never tires of visiting. Most of them are well known for being at the top of the culinary world, some of them are interesting newcomers, and all of them transcend quality in so many areas and look as magnificent in real life as they do on the printed page.

Spectacular Restaurants of Texas serves as your guide to a wide range of cuisines, concepts and styles all over the Lone Star State. As you flip through these pages, I hope you'll find a restaurant that is perfect for your next occasion. I can promise you this: You're sure to be impressed with the lush photography that captures Texas' finest. You'll be dazzeled to discover the national acclaim that restaurants in Fort Worth, Austin, Houston, San Antonio, and, of course, Dallas continuously enjoy.

All the best,

John Carpenter

PS. I like to know what to wear to a restaurant I've never been at before, I have included a tip from the restaurateurs themselves as to what is appropriate for their establishments.

Austin

Fort Worth

Dallas

Contents

Jeffrey's Restaurant and Bar, page 23

CHAPTER ONE
AUSTIN

ABOVE Garden entrance to Aquarelle Restaurant Français.

RIGHT Hot chocolate soufflé cake with orange sauce Suzette.

AQUARELLE RESTAURANT FRANÇAIS

Teresa Wilson, chef/managing partner

Robert Brady, chef/managing partner

The details are what make a meal at Aquarelle Restaurant Français exquisite. Excellence is achieved by paying attention to the little things that, when taken not in part but together, produce a favorable and memorable experience. Aquarelle's award-winning cuisine; professional, attentive service; classic French table appointments; and romantic ambiance combine to create a formula that keeps patrons yearning for a repeat interlude.

Chefs Teresa Wilson and Robert Brady conceived their idea of the restaurant in 1995 while working at the Michelin Guide-rated restaurant Les Frères Lani in Aix-en-Provence, France. The plans for the restaurant did not come to fruition until they purchased a turn-of-the-century house in the heart of downtown Austin in 1999. Together they embarked on what is still the city's only

authentic French gastronomic establishment and what has been consistently voted year after year as one of Austin's best and most romantic five-star restaurants.

At Aquarelle, Wilson and Brady create contemporary Franco-American cuisine using the highest-quality ingredients, whether produce or cheeses from local farms or imported snails and fresh duck foie gras from France. The menu changes seasonally to take advantage of what's fresh and abundant. Culinary highlights have included wild Burgundy escargot fricassee with oregano-garlic butter, olive tapenade-stuffed saddle of rabbit, blanquette of Atlantic halibut with littleneck clams, herbed goat cheese torte with roasted pear tomatoes, and pan-seared duck foie gras with caramelized apples and cider foam. Desserts are not to be missed: the warm Rainier cherry clafoutis, pistachio

TOP LEFT Fricassée of wild Burgundy snails with oregano-garlic butter.

TOP RIGHT Atlantic salmon fillet over creamed French green lentils with apple-wood smoked bacon gastrique.

BOTTOM LEFT Chefs Robert Brady and Teresa Wilson.

BOTTOM RIGHT One of Aquarelle's decadent desserts which keep guests coming back for more.

ABOVE The staff of Aquarelle Restaurant Français.

ice cream-stuffed profiteroles with hot chocolate sauce, and the signature chocolate soufflé cake with orange sauce Suzette and house-made vanilla ice cream never disappoint. And with more than 100 selections, a large portion of which is dedicated to interesting and affordable vin de pays (French country wines), Aquarelle's wine list offers something to suit even the most discerning palate.

Complementing the cuisine is the design and decor of the 100-year-old house. Wilson and Brady wanted to capture the feeling and ambiance of a country bastide in the south of France, offering a warm and unpretentious atmosphere. Double good luck fell upon Aquarelle during the restoration of the space.

First, when good friend and architect David Hurst, now president of Integrated Builders in Dallas, accepted the job of redesigning and orchestrating the renovation. Hurst's professional expertise in state-of-the-art kitchen design and layout, which included the installation of a custom cooking suite, gave the chefs the proper tools to produce the cuisine they envisioned.

The second bit of good fortune came when master carpenter Michael "Otto" Much offered his artistic skills to recreate the beauty of the old home. Much's craftsmanship and guidance is visible in every corner of the restaurant. Patrons are served in a relaxed-formal setting of soft, warm hues; handmade European tapestries; French lace curtains; crisp linens; shaded table candle-lamps; imported flatware; and custom china–all of which accent Aquarelle's artistic food preparations.

What to wear: Business casual.

More About Teresa & Robert ...

Who has had the biggest influence on your career?
Jacques Pepin and Julia Childs. They made it easy to understand the techniques of French cuisine.

What do you like most about doing business in Texas?
Taking care of Texans, who know what they like but are seldom averse to trying something new or different.

What is the most unique/impressive/beautiful restaurant in which you've dined in Texas?
The French Room in Dallas. Just go there–you will understand why.

What is one thing most people don't know about you?
We are not married!

Aquarelle Restaurant Français
606 Rio Grande
Austin, TX 78701
512-479-8117
www.aquarellerestaurant.com

ABOVE Chef Mario Montana, Manager Luis Patino and Chef Margarito Machado are serving up "Old World" charm and cuisine that says "amore" in every bite.

RIGHT Carmelo's open air piazza features al fresco dining, old oak trees and "Adickes-men" statues in the fountains. These Italian troubadours are the work of famed Houston sculptor David Adickes.

CARMELO'S RISTORANTE

Carmelo Mauro, proprietor

It's a steamy August day, and Carmelo Mauro and his wife, Hilary, are at New York's JFK airport, waiting on a plane that will take them to their European homeland. After 20 years of working in restaurants and hotels all over the world, Mauro moved to Houston and opened Carmelo's Ristorante in 1981. Four years later, he expanded to Austin, locating in the state's oldest standing train depot. "When I first saw it, with its thick stone walls, it reminded me so much of my hometown in Italy," Mauro remembers.

He's speaking of the Mediterranean town of Taormina, and the charming Carmelo's aims to re-create the magic of the famed Sicilian resort. Good food, art, and music combine to accomplish that goal and draw people in not just for dinner but for all kinds of special occasions.

The authentic Italian menu and wine list is complemented by the music of accordionist Herschel Moody, who performs six nights a week in the role of a strolling street musician. Mauro also collects and displays throughout Carmelo's the works of artists Herb Mears and David Adickes, including the latter's Italian troubadours, designed for the outdoor fountain in the restaurant's open air piazza.

Taking care of guests while Mauro is abroad is General Manager Luis Patino, who's been at Carmelo's for 25 years. Patino is a pro at ensuring that customers are treated "as if they are dining in your home," Mauro says. "And what do you do when friends come to your home? You roll out the red carpet. You welcome them with a big hug. You serve the best. You create a

memory. That's how we run our restaurant." (And since 2001, he's been advising the next generation of restaurateurs to do the same by way of a Carmelo's built on the campus of Del Valle High School, where students learn restaurant management and operations in a real-world setting.)

What to wear: "There's no dress code. People should feel at home when they come and dine with us," Mauro says.

LEFT TOP The Tara Room is the lightest and brightest room, decorated with flowers, memorabilia and antique tapestry to accommodate 30-42 people with an excellent view overlooking the courtyard.

LEFT BOTTOM Renowned for romantic candlelit dinners, Carmelo's has always been the perfect place to "pop the question," or for planning bridal showers, rehearsal dinners, weddings and receptions.

ABOVE Carmelo's Ristorante is located in the historic Old Depot Hotel, the oldest standing train depot in Texas. Built in 1872, the "Railroad House" accommodated passengers traveling to other railroads and four stagecoach lines.

MORE ABOUT CARMELO ...

What is one thing most people don't know about you?
"I worked my way up in the hotel business from bellhop to general manager."

Who has had the most impact on your career?
"My mother, Antonina. She would spend most of the day in the kitchen cooking."

To what do you attribute your success?
"Perseverance. High energy. Immense love of the business. The most important thing is to believe in yourself, know what you are doing, and surround yourself with people who believe in and want to grow with you," he says. "The rest just follows."

Carmelo's Ristorante
504 East Fifth Street
Austin, TX 78701
512-477-7497
www.carmelosrestaurant.com

ABOVE The colorful main dining room reflects the spirit of the tropics and opens onto the shaded patio with fountains and lush plantings.

RIGHT Diners at Doña Emilia's enjoy New Latin entreés like Coffee-Crusted Tenderloin with Grilled Shrimp as well as more traditional South American dishes. The restaurant features a carefully selected list of fine South American wines and Latin cocktails.

DOÑA EMILIA'S SOUTH AMERICAN BAR & GRILL

Howard Kells, Stuart Rowe, Ruben Cuero and Emilia Hurtado, partners

Embodying classic Latin elegance in form and substance, Doña Emilia's South American Bar & Grill introduced upscale South American cuisine to the diners of Central Texas. Partners Howard Kells, an Austin designer/builder, and Ruben Cuero, who brought to the table the culinary traditions of his native Columbia, combined their considerable talents to create an extraordinary fine dining experience in downtown Austin.

The restaurant comprises two levels and 6,000 square feet of bold architecture and festive decor. Venetian marble plastered walls, a soaring atrium, and an outdoor patio with water fountains compliment the South American cuisine. With an eye toward Austin's commitment to protecting the environment, Kells created a green restaurant, from recycled glass countertops in the bars to bamboo hardwood floors throughout. Expansive,

full-length windows on both levels extend the diners' experience of this relaxing tropical setting. Adding to the sensual atmosphere, pastel-colored lights flood the walls with subtly changing color.

Serving traditional South American dishes like Ropa Vieja, as well as New Latin interpretations like Coffee-Crusted Tenderloin and Chilean Sea Bass with Habañero Soy Sauce, the restaurant has been lauded by food critics and is patronized by a broad base of food enthusiasts.

What to wear: Typically, dinner guests dress in cocktail or casual evening attire suitable for dancing. Daytime guests wear dressy casual and business casual clothing.

Doña Emilia's South American Bar & Grill
"Explore a New Continent of Fun and Flavor"
101 San Jacinto Boulevard
Austin, TX 78701
512-478-2520
www.donaemilias.com

ABOVE The Driskill Grill provides sophistication in a laid-back atmosphere. Paneled walls, cut-glass mirrors, and portraits of Texas Governors Ma and Pa Ferguson offer a true Texas feel.

RIGHT The Driskill Grill is located within the opulent Driskill Hotel, located in downtown Austin in the heart of the business, entertainment, and historic districts.

THE DRISKILL GRILL

David J. Bull, executive chef

Dining at the award-winning Driskill Grill—as celebrities, dignitaries, and socialites often do—guests experience the culinary philosophy of executive chef David J. Bull. "Food is an art form that lasts only a few minutes, so we have to keep standards high. I am never content to bend the rules concerning the food that comes out of the kitchen. We strive for perfection, and I am as stubborn as necessary to ensure that our guests are served only the best." Bull lightly adds, "I guess my name really fits. Bulls are known for being stubborn."

The menu at The Driskill Grill features inventive dishes: charred beef tenderloin with black truffle-potato puree and pan-seared Copper River salmon with English peas and chanterelle mushrooms. And though the food is sophisticated, the atmosphere is down-to-earth. "Stuffy is out. Pretentious is out," Bull says. "It is a privilege to be a part of people's lives, creating memories, sharing in their special occasions. We pride ourselves in that privilege. When people leave happy, we have done our job."

What to wear: Austin is a particularly laid-back town. Doing business in Texas means that everyone is always welcome just as they are, whether entertaining clients, coming in after a long day outside, or enjoying a romantic dinner for two.

The Driskill Grill
604 Brazos Street
Austin, TX 78701
512-391-7162
www.criskillgrill.com

ABOVE One of four intimate dining rooms.

RIGHT Crispy oysters on yucca root chips.

JEFFREY'S RESTAURANT & BAR

Ron Weiss, operating partner
David Garrido, executive chef

"Someone once asked me to describe Jeffrey's in a word," says Ron Weiss. "The first one that came to mind was 'alchemy.' For dining to be exceptional, everything has to work together in a way that can't quite be explained."

Though Jeffrey's has for 30 years left diners speechless with its masterful take on Southwestern and Latin tastes, industry experts haven't been at a loss for words. Dishes like oysters on yucca root chips with habanero honey aioli, chilled corn soup with smoked salmon and pea coulis, and beef tenderloin with pecorino rosemary potatoes and wild mushroom brandy sauce have given them plenty to talk about.

Jeffrey's Restaurant and executive chef David Garrido have been recognized by the *Distinguished Restaurants of North America, Wine Spectator, Gourmet, Bon Appétit, The New York Times*, The James Beard House, and others for culinary ingenuity and warm hospitality. Weiss says "We never forget that it's our guests who truly have the last word." And the distinguished list of patrons includes presidents past and present, governors, celebrities, socialites, and regular folks who know good food.

What to wear: Jackets aren't required, but people do like to dress up.

Jeffrey's Restaurant & Bar
1204 West Lynn Street
Austin, TX 78703
512-477-5584
www.jeffreysofaustin.com

LEFT The upscale bistro atmosphere and the casual European ambience is a result of the owner's attention to detail.

ABOVE One of the four private dining rooms for parties that prefer private rooms.

LOUIE'S 106

Joe Elmiger, proprietor
Norbert Brandt, executive chef

Executive chef Norbert Brandt describes the look and feel of his restaurant, Louie's 106, as "timeless," and, indeed, the celebrated Spanish eatery has changed little in nearly 25 years. Its location is enviable: downtown Austin, in the heart of the city's entertainment district. And with a warm, clubby vibe and sophisticated New York-style decor, Louie's has been a staple of the local dining scene since 1986.

The diverse menu, says owner Joe Elmiger, is the restaurant's strength and reason for its continued popularity. Tapas have become ubiquitous in recent years, but they've long been served at Louie's, and they underscore the Mediterranean flavor of the restaurant. Guests love that they can sample tuna carpaccio with fire-roasted naan bread, chargrilled beef, and Morraccan barbecued shrimp all on one plate.

Lunch and dinner feature daily specials from the rotisserie, as well as pastas, risottos, bouillabaisse, grilled vegetables, and salads. Favorites include paella Valencia, with chicken, sausage, fish, shrimp, mussels, and saffron rice; pan-seared, pumpkin-seed crusted red snapper served on a casserole of seafood, cannelini beans, and gnocchi; and Moroccan-spiced pork tenderloin medallions with Gruyere mashed potatoes and honey Dijon mustard sauce.

Wine lovers are right at home at the six-time recipient of the Wine Spectator Award of Excellence. More than 400 labels guarantee a perfect match, no matter which of Brandt's dishes one chooses.

What to wear: The phrase "casual chic" says it all.

Louie's 106
106 East Sixth Street
Austin, TX 78701
512-476-1998
www.louies106.net

ABOVE Eclectic Game Lodge entrance greets guests at Ranch 616.

RIGHT Ranch 616's name welcomes guests with an exterior custom 100-foot neon rattlesnake design by famed artist Bob "Daddy-O" Wade.

RANCH 616

Kevin Williamson, chef and proprietor
Antonio Vidal, co-chef

The press has called Ranch 616 a "diner gone designer," a Texas-style diner worthy of Manhattan, and a place "you can make your own." But those who eat there regularly (and there are many) simply call it "The Ranch."

With a nod to the South Texas ice house and flavors from the Texas-Mexico border area ("not Tex-Mex," chef/owner Kevin Williamson emphasizes), The Ranch is at once fabulous and laid-back, upscale without a pretentious brick in the building, proving that sophisticated food isn't exclusive to uptight, white-tablecloth restaurants. Unique in the world, there is no other spot quite like The Ranch. Likewise, there's no one quite like Williamson.

After stints in real estate and on Wall Street, Williamson, a native Texan, found his place in the kitchen. With stops in La Jolla, California, New York City, and Aspen, Colorado (where he helped open the renowned Ajax Tavern), Williamson returned to cook in his native Austin. He spent two years at the original Central Market before opening Ranch 616 in 1998. With expert assistance from Antonio Vidal, the kitchen turns out mouthwatering steak and seafood specials (the Black Angus rib eye comes topped with a fried egg; grass-fed Longhorn beef has the unique taste of free-range meat), as well as crowd-pleasers like homemade tamales and fish tacos.

At Ranch 616, Williamson's Texas pride is evident at every turn. The restaurant's decor spins on the murals of local artist Bob "Daddy-O" Wade, the menu hinges on Gulf seafood and Texas beef and wine, and the service is always fast and friendly.

What to wear: The dress code is "Austin informal."

Ranch 616
616 Nueces Street
Austin, TX 78701
512-479-7616

ABOVE Ringside at Sullivan's Steakhouse in the infamous warehouse district of downtown Austin offers the city's hottest live jazz and leading dance bands. Sullivan's Steakhouse is known as a one-stop entertainment destination.

RIGHT Sullivan's 1940's-styled steakhouse offers an extensive martini list. House favorite is the vodka-infused fresh pineapple "Knock-Out" martini.

FAR RIGHT Austin's Sullivan's Steakhouse is the flagship of a successful concept that has expanded to fifteen locations and is on the move.

SULLIVAN'S STEAKHOUSE
OF AUSTIN

Swank is the word at Sullivan's Steakhouse, a one-stop destination for fine dining and lively entertainment. The 1940's-styled steakhouse features the juiciest steaks and freshest seafood, skillfully-poured martinis, and great live jazz. And the restaurant continually wins awards from *Wine Spectator* magazine for its superb wine list.

In an impeccably-appointed dining room with attentive servers at hand, well-heeled diners enjoy hand-selected, certified Angus beef such as the restaurant's signature steak: the 20-ounce bone-in Kansas City Strip, live Maine lobster and fresh-daily seafood.

After dessert, live music beckons. In the cozy bar, flush with grand pianos, high-end cognacs, single malt scotches, an incredible selection of wine and a fully-stocked cigar humidor, there's live jazz. In the Ringside Lounge, cocktails flow, and the city's leading dance bands keep the energy moving.

Austin's Sullivan's Steakhouse is the restaurant's flagship; the concept has expanded to 15 cities across the United States, and expansion to new cities continues.

A "playground for adults," the restaurant is a hot spot where all sorts of people can indulge their dining and entertaining desires, from the high-powered executive hosting a power lunch to the professional who enjoys a networking happy hour to a couple out for a romantic night on the town. *Nation's Restaurant News* says, "Don't tell the pleasure police about Sullivan's Steakhouse." But judging from the crowds, everyone else already knows.

What to wear: Sullivan's is a place where the beautiful people sip and sup and they dress casually, but well, beautifully.

Sullivan's Steakhouse of Austin
300 Colorado Street, #200
Austin, TX 78701
512-495-6504
www.sullivansteakhouse.com

Fort Worth Chop House, page 43

CHAPTER TWO
FORT WORTH

BISTRO LOUISE

Louise Lamensdorf, executive chef and proprietor

Dressed in sunny yellow with touches of bright blue, the multiaward-winning Bistro Louise is as charming as its proprietor, Louise Lamensdorf. And its menu, rife with the flavors and techniques of France, Italy, and Spain, caters to the palates of the well-traveled patrons who dine here.

Though her restaurant, like the established Fort Worth neighborhoods nearby, is more classic than trendy, Lamensdorf says that the secret to success is staying abreast of current styles. She travels to Europe at least every other year to work in a Michelin Guide-rated starred restaurant. And she has only just returned from a 10-day trip to New York, where she dined at Jean Georges, Yumcha, Davidburke & Donatella, and other famed eateries. "When chefs go to restaurants, they learn about what other chefs are doing," she says. "Such things play into our ability to evolve."

New dishes include a buffalo steak with barley risotto and currant sauce and a rare ivory salmon. "But there are some things," she says, "that people just can't live without—like the soft shell crab almondine, a nod to my Louisiana roots."

What to wear: Dress neither up nor down—I like to call the dress code Fort Worth casual.

Bistro Louise
Stonegate Commons
2900 South Hulen Street, Suite 40
Fort Worth, TX 76109
817-922-9244
www.bistrolouise.com

TOP Mouthwatering Redfish and Shrimp Ceviche Campechana.

RIGHT Bonnell's features an Award-Winning Wine List.

BONNELL'S FINE TEXAS CUISINE

Jon Bonnell, executive chef and proprietor

To say that Jon Bonnell, just back from a family vacation and on his way to New York to cook at The James Beard House for a second time, is busy is an understatement. Likewise, it's tough to overestimate his passion for his Texas roots: They are the foundation of his namesake restaurant, Bonnell's Fine Texas Cuisine. "I use every local farm and ranch that I can. When I find a new one, I add something to the menu," he says.

Hill Country venison, South Texas quail, free-range chicken from Denison, and grass-fed beef from Grandview are part of his culinary arsenal, which also includes Gulf Coast seafood, such as redfish and oysters, and emphasizes organic products. And from the time he opened the doors in

2001, Bonnell has been knocking folks dead with mouthwatering interpretations of them all.

Always a promising scholar, his success came as a surprise to none. One of only two students to graduate with honors from the New England Culinary Institute in 1997, Bonnell began his professional chef career as an intern in the kitchen at Mr. B's Bistro in New Orleans French Quarter. (He'd been stirring up stovetop magic at home for years.) He then returned to his hometown and spent two years at Randall's Gourmet Restaurant and Cheesecakery before leaving to plan his own restaurant. In the interim, he helped open Escargot and worked as a personal chef.

It didn't take long for Bonnell, now 35, to catch the eye of local and national critics, who continually praise his efforts. He was the winner of the 2004 Dallas Wine and Food Festival chef's competition and was named Texas Restaurant Association's Outstanding Restaurateur for the same year. Appetizers like shrimp and redfish ceviche marinated in lime juice, served with tomatoes, chilies, and fresh avocado; and entrees like grilled boar chops with blackberry-rum demiglace and baby vegetables keep tongues wagging and diners burning a trail to his off-the-beaten-path door.

And through it all, the modest man in the kitchen has remained grounded. He's hands-on in the kitchen and on hand to meet and greet guests with a shy, sincere smile. Soft-spoken and humble, he maintains a strict policy of treating everyone from the wealthiest customer to the newest dishwasher with respect and dignity.

"Never pretend that you are better than anyone else," he says. Never worry about someone stealing your recipes might be another of his rules: "I give away all of my recipes."

As refined and unpretentious as Bonnell himself, the restaurant's upscale ranch house-style dining room recently got a makeover, with antler chandeliers, saddle leather accents, and mahogany-finished wood to freshen its understated Western look. Everything else the friendly service, the down-home sophistication, the to-die-for green chili cheese grits remains the same.

What to wear: "I call it Fort Worth fancy. That means come in your best boots and jeans," he says "And come hungry."

LEFT Texas-style Bruschetta with Carmelized 1015 Onions, Avocado and Pecan Relish, Fire-roasted Salsa and Deborah Rogers' Goat Cheese.

RIGHT Broken Arrow Ranch Axis Venison Carpaccio with Creamy Green Peppercorn Drizzle.

Q&A

MORE ABOUT JON ...

What is the highest compliment you've received professionally?

In 2004, after dinner at the James Beard House, the staff said ours was the best-received meal in memory. I was asked to return to cook again in 2005.

What personal indulgence do you spend the most money on?

Wine, fly-fishing, and photography.

What business philosophy have you stuck to for years that still works today?

Do what you do best, with the most passion and energy that you can and never settle for mediocrity.

What do you like most about doing business in Texas?

Texans are the most neighborly people in the world. Employees feel more like family and customers more like friends.

Bonnell's Fine Texas Cuisine
4259 Bryant Irvin Road
Fort Worth, TX 76109
817-738-5489
www.bonnellsrestaurant.com

ABOVE Chef Hans with chocolate soufflé signature dessert.

FACING PAGE TOP Chilled Shrimp with avocado sauce.

FACING PAGE BOTTOM Sliced breast of duck with savory sauce.

FAR RIGHT Main entrance of penthouse dining room.

Jean-Claude Adam fell in love with the friendly people of Texas 25 years ago. Likewise, the people of Texas were romanced by the charm of the Arlington restaurant he and executive chef Hans Bergmann opened in 1986. The pair worked together in Europe before partnering on Cacharel, where they've successfully combined their expert abilities.

Nine stories in the sky, the restaurant is known for its panoramic view and cozy French Country atmosphere. An amiable host, Adam is almost always on hand to greet guests and escort them to their tables, while the talented Bergmann prepares traditional French cuisine with skill and inventive flair. His sautéed filet of Norwegian salmon with a champagne-dill sauce, sliced roasted breast of duck with a cassis sauce, and grilled veal T-bone with a Provençal sauce with chanterelle mushrooms are fantastique.

The wine list is a solid mix from various regions; selections have been handpicked to complement the fine French favorites as well as the "Beef Eaters" menu, perfectly grilled cuts for steak connoisseurs served with either peppercorn or Cabernet Sauvignon sauce.

And no meal is complete without dessert. Crème brulée is a popular choice, but nothing beats the thrill of a hot-from-the-oven soufflé. In flavors like mango, hazelnut, Grand Marnier, and, of course, chocolate and served with fresh whipped cream, they are irresistible.

What to wear: Some often dress for a special occasion, but sophisticated casual clothes are fine.

Cacharel
2221 East Lamar Boulevard
Brookhollow Tower Two, Ninth Floor
Arlington, TX 76006
817-640-9981
www.cacharel.net

ABOVE Walking distance from the Convention Center and minutes from Sundance Square, Del Frisco's is Fort Worth's favorite downtown steakhouse.

FACING PAGE LEFT The cornerstone of Del Frisco's Double Eagle Steak House's award-winning menu is USDA Prime Beef and cold water Australian Lobster tails.

FACING PAGE RIGHT With a wine inventory of 10,000 bottles from across the world, Del Frisco's bar is the "in spot" for business networking, romantic interludes and celebrity sightings.

DEL FRISCO'S DOUBLE EAGLE
STEAK HOUSE FORT WORTH

Adam Jones, general manager
Martin Thompson, executive chef

Founded a century ago on cattle, oil, and the Wild West, Fort Worth today is a sophisticated arts and culinary jewel. Helping the city blaze a trail to the top of the fine dining scene is Del Frisco's, located in an historical building in the heart of the city's downtown and a destination steakhouse for a decade.

White tablecloths, dark wood, polished brass, alabaster lighting, and walls decked with photos of "great people who live and dine in Fort Worth, create a vibe that's cosmopolitan but not pretentious," says General Manager Adam Jones. Executive Chef Martin Thompson delivers USDA prime steaks, Australian cold water lobster tails with seafood features such as pecan-crusted halibut with orange beurre

blanc and seared sea bass with roasted red bell pepper sauce changing daily.

The restaurant's million-dollar wine inventory includes 10,000 bottles of the finest selections from all regions of the world. It's housed beneath the dining room in a cellar lined with limestone from the original 1890 building. The mezzanine bar draws a refined crowd of business executives looking to unwind, relax, and enjoy premium cocktails.

What to wear: The atmosphere is always comfortable and casual. You see a lot of jeans, starched white shirts and business suits. No one ever feels out of place.

Del Frisco's Double Eagle Steak House Fort Worth
812 Main Street
Fort Worth, TX 76102
817-877-3999
www.delfriscos.com

ABOVE The dining room at Fort Worth Chophouse gives a nod to the city's roots with its Western chic decor.

RIGHT Bourbon flows in the Chophouse bar.

FORT WORTH CHOPHOUSE

Doug Cox, general manager

Time was that Fort Worth's Sundance Square was home to Wild West outlaws and rabble-rousing mischief makers. Today, however, the historic venue offers a wide array of entertainment and appeals to those looking for an afternoon or evening of arts, culture, fun, and an award-winning meal. That's where the Fort Worth Chophouse comes in.

Part of the M Crowd fine dining empire that includes Mi Cocina, Taco Diner, The Mercury Grill and Mainstream Fish House, the upscale steakhouse serves thick, juicy steaks and succulent seafood, taking a gourmet approach to every dish, whether pepper-crusted beef, double-cut pork chop, broiled halibut, grilled chicken, or lamb with mint jelly. Potatoes are served five flavorful ways and homemade condiments like the jalapeno

and grilled garlic sauce make every bite extraordinary. The wine collection boasts interesting selections from around the world, and the bar mixes premium cocktails.

In an inviting, classic steakhouse setting, diners enjoy impeccable service. Whether discussing business over lunch, celebrating the end of a workday with happy hour at the bustling bar, or settling in for a romantic pre-theater dinner, guests can count on consistently great cuisine and just the right amount of attention from the seasoned waitstaff.

What to wear: Jeans, boots, and fashionably chic attire are de rigueur in Cowtown.

Fort Worth Chophouse
301 South Main Street
Fort Worth, TX 76102
817-336-4129
www.mcrowd.com

ABOVE Gunsmoke Grill's Victorian bar make for a comfortable yet lavish experience while enjoying their signature White Citroen Cosmopolitan.

RIGHT Chef Keith Hicks' specialty and guest favorite: Prime Bone-in Ribeye with crisp onion strings over truffle oil-infused smashed potatoes and grilled asparagus with basil-infused olive oil.

FAR RIGHT Warm, polished interior design set the stage for a great meal.

GUNSMOKE GRILL AND SALOON

April Simpson, proprietor

A massive antique bar sets the tone at Fort Worth's Gunsmoke Grill and Saloon. A remarkable piece from the 19th century, the long, polished bar evokes in a single glance the rich history of the Old West. Surrounded by bordello-red walls, scarlet curtains, and a pressed-tin ceiling, were it not for contemporary touches, you might think you'd been transported back in time. Owner April Simpson calls the look "rustic Victorian." And it is truly unique in the city.

Quintessential Cowtown but more than just another candlelit steakhouse, Gunsmoke has been noted for its striking decor and climate-controlled alfresco dining, but the food is what garners the most reaction. Executive chef Keith Hicks' menu drew quick acclaim when the restaurant opened in July 2004. Within a few months, *Dallas Morning News* had awarded Gunsmoke four stars, the *Fort Worth Star-Telegram* called it a "beef bull's eye," and *Texas Monthly* proclaimed the bone-in rib-eye "divine."

Nowhere else will you find Hicks' jalapeño beef with a cucumber-red onion salad with Asian vinaigrette, Double-cut pork chop with jalapeño-cheese grits and prickly pear puree, or ancho chipotle short ribs with southwestern couscous carbonara. Four-cheese macaroni and smashed potatoes with white truffle oil are outstanding renditions of classics. "It's comfort food with a twist" explains Director of Operations Joche Westmoreland. "This is 'cravable' food." Westmoreland's diverse wine list, awarded "Best of Fort Worth" by *Fort Worth Weekly*, compliments the menu perfectly and is organized under the six national flags that have flown over Texas.

What to wear: "The dress is business casual, and jeans are acceptable," Westmoreland says.

Gunsmoke Grill and Saloon
3105 Cockrell Avenue
Fort Worth, TX 76109
817-920-0833
www.gunsmokegrill.com

ABOVE View from the private entrance to the Lonesome Dove Western Bistro.

RIGHT The Lonesome Dove's signature dish; roasted garlic stuffed beef tenderloin with western plaid hash, grilled asparagus and syrah demi-glace.

THE LONESOME DOVE
WESTERN BISTRO

Tim Love, executive chef and proprietor

The moment you walk through the doors at The Lonesome Dove Western Bistro you know it's extraordinary. The tiny, dimly lit restaurant has a soft, natural feel that at once wraps you in warmth and sends a little shiver up your spine. No doubt about it–Tim Love's Restaurant is a special place.

In the kitchen since college, Love opened Lonesome Dove in June 2000 in a building in the Historic Fort Worth Stockyards and began serving Urban Western cuisine. "Southwestern was too limiting," the 33-year-old Love says.

"I wanted to encompass all the ingredients and cultures of the Old West. I wanted to exploit the game and produce native to this area and to elevate ranch food to city standards. What we do is comfortable but dressed up." In other words, it's basic but beautiful, like the mouthwatering braised lamb shank with fresh ricotta and fried spinach, for example.

Love and his wife, Emilie, invested everything they had into Lonesome Dove, and their risk was fast rewarded. The restaurant quickly rose to the top of the dining scene, not only in Fort Worth but also nationwide. Food

writers from *The New York Times*, *Bon Appétit*, *Esquire*, *Southern Living*, and many others have raved time and again about the cooking cowboy, who helped put his beloved hometown on the culinary map.

"I want people to think of Fort Worth for food, not just museums and longhorns," says the Texas-born-and-bred chef called "a rising star of American cuisine" by The James Beard House.

And so it is. The Food Network recently aired "Cowboys on the Trail," which followed Love's 2004 culinary expedition to California. Zagat awarded Lonesome Dove a coveted spot in its 2005 edition of *America's Top Restaurants*. But perhaps the greatest indicator of all: Local regulars and visitors from afar claim all the bar seating, fill the 14 tables, and keep the three private dining rooms booked every night.

What to wear: Boots and jeans are de rigueur. Then again, so are suits, you just won't see many of them.

FACING PAGE TOP LEFT Truffled tuna tartar on black bean purée with fried winter greens.

FACING PAGE TOP RIGHT The Dove Lease, one of three private dining rooms at the Lonesome Dove Western Bistro.

FACING PAGE BOTTOM LEFT A table setting in the Dove Lease for a rehearsal dinner.

FACING PAGE BOTTOM RIGHT Fruit Fireworks, a dessert favorite of a caramel apple with merengue wrapped fresh fruit and candied walnuts.

ABOVE The Urban-Western inspired main dining room of the Lonesome Dove Western Bistro.

MORE FROM TIM ...

What are people surprised to learn about you?
When Emilie and I opened Lonesome Dove, we were sweating. We had $1,000 left in the bank—that's it.

What's the highest compliment you've received professionally?
I was the first Fort Worth chef to be invited to cook at the James Beard House in New York.

Lonesome Dove Western Bistro
2406 North Main Street
Fort Worth, TX 76106
817-740-8810
www.lonesomedovebistro.com

TOP Sonoma Dining Room during an afternoon sunset.

FACING PAGE LEFT Pan-Seared Ahi Tuna.

FACING PAGE MIDDLE Crab Stuffed Sea Bass.

FACING PAGE RIGHT Pepper Crusted Rack of Lamb.

SONOMA GRILL & WINE BAR

Jan Zwerver, proprietor

"Three kinds of art shine through," Jan Zwerver says of a dining experience at his Sonoma Grill & Wine Bar, which he opened with his wife, Kim, three years ago. "Original oil paintings by Richard Nunez fill the walls. Dishes are prepared in a manner that takes the culinary experience to a new level. And winemaking is an art form all its own." This "trilogy of art," as the 39-year-old gourmand calls it, is behind everything at the chic neighborhood restaurant.

The space is bright and airy; the ambiance is easy. Selections from the substantial wine list are available by the bottle, half bottle, glass, or flight. General Manager Victor Rojas is there to guide you and provide the perfect juice for your palate. And the food, prepared by chefs Ben Benetiz and

Ryan Bridges, is California dreamy. Sea bass stuffed with lump crabmeat, seared ahi tuna marinated in red curry, and filet medallions topped with a shiraz reduction and gorgonzola are hard-to-beat favorites.

Sonoma has a je ne sais quoi common in the valley for which it is named. It's something you can't quite put your finger on. It's a certain kind of joy that makes you want to linger.

What to wear. Sonoma is a California-centric restaurant and the guests dress accordingly. Camp shirts, shorts, and fashionable jeans are all fine.

Sonoma Grill & Wine Bar
380 Parker Square
Flower Mound, TX 75028
972-899-8989
www.sonomagrillandwinebar.com
Design and Construction by Bill Hood, Construction Concepts Corp., Irving, TX

CHAPTER THREE
DALLAS

ABOVE Bold architectural features combined with natural materials, vivid color and exceptional contemporary art all unite to form the main dining room.

RIGHT A geometric design motif is adapted in metal and glass throughout the bar area.

ABACUS

Kent Rathbun, executive chef and proprietor

Kent Rathbun exudes the kind of energy common to those who spend every day doing what they love, and what the 44-year-old loves to do is entertain. "It's the best part of being a chef," he says. "You're always at a party." Or, in Rathbun's case, you're always the host of the party.

Entertaining comes naturally to the gregarious Missouri native, who grew up in a family who knew how to make sure guests are having a great time. And at Abacus, people come to do just that. Whether impressing a date, marking a memorable wedding anniversary, celebrating a job promotion, or raising a glass to retirement, Abacus is the ideal five-star dining destination. But that's not to say that the legendary lobster shooters aren't perfect for an ordinary Tuesday night.

Since its opening in 1999, menu items like lobster shooters and sushi have demonstrated Rathbun's inventive approach in the kitchen. He brings the flavors of the Mediterranean, American, Southwest and Pacific Rim influences together in unexpected ways.

Guests who want to watch the master at work can gather a group of eight to twelve and book the chef's table for a view of Dallas' first European-style theater kitchen. Now that's entertainment! For special events they also have private dining and offer off-site catering.

What to wear: Abacus is not necessarily a coat-and-tie restaurant, though most people do dress up. "Our only dress code is no denim," says Rathbun. "We won't ask you to leave, but we will ask you to sit in the bar."

FACING PAGE TOP Dallas' first European-style theatre kitchen

FACING PAGE BOTTOM A sleek, semi-private dining room may be curtained off for special events.

RIGHT The Chef's table allows guests to interact with Chef Rathbun and enjoy special tastings.

Q&A

MORE ABOUT
KENT ...

Who has had the biggest impact on your career?
I've been extremely fortunate to work with a lot of great chefs in some of the best restaurants. However, Jim Mills, now general manager at the Houstonian Hotel, always stays top-of-mind. Jim taught me a tremendous amount about food and balance and how to really refine the taste of a sauce or marinade. Even more than cooking, Jim also advised me on how to get others to listen to me, respect me and negotiate business politics.

What color best describes you?
Yellow. I'm not afraid to stand out.

What is the highest compliment you've received professionally?
Jacques Pépin came into Abacus one day and after finishing his dinner, he said to me, "Can you imagine where chefs would be today if we'd been serving food like this in the 1980s?"

Abacus
4511 McKinney Avenue
Dallas, TX 75205
214-559-3111
www.abacus-restaurant.com

ABOVE Classic decor at Café Pacific provides a
backdrop for fine wines, fresh seafood and Prime steaks.

RIGHT The bar at Café Pacific draws a who's who of
Dallas.

CAFÉ PACIFIC

Brian Campbell, executive chef

At Café Pacific, fresh flowers, white linens, marble floors, rich wood paneling, and etched glass create a sophisticated environment. For 25 years, such elegance has provided a backdrop for the fine wines, the fresh seafood, and the prime steaks. These are combined with an impressive level of service expected by the city's prominent business and social leaders, making Café Pacific a Park Cities powerhouse.

As executive chef Brian Campbell explains it: "We do whatever it takes to please the customer. I think this philosophy has been practiced at every successful restaurant that I have been involved with, and it is definitely the theory behind Café Pacific." A member of the *Nation's Restaurant News* Fine Dining Hall of Fame, a recipient of the Distinguished Restaurants of North American Fine Dining Award, and selected Dallas' number one seafood restaurant by Zagat, Café Pacific is widely recognized as a premier foodie destination in the Southwest. Area residents, who never tire of going there, agree.

What to wear: People in the Park Cities know fashion. The dress code is upscale; coats not required, but usually worn in the evening; and jeans, shorts, or collarless shirts are not seated.

Café Pacific
24 Highland Park Village
Dallas, TX 75205
214-526-1170

ABOVE Absolut Peppar® vodka cocktail sauce and remoulade give Blue Crab Cakes a Texas kick.

TOP LEFT River rock fireplaces and handmade chandeliers adorn the main dining room.

TOP RIGHT Open since 1998, Cool River is a Las Colinas landmark.

COOL RIVER

Robert Stephenson, executive chef

Ask Bob Stephenson to share his recipe for artichoke stuffing or recite an original poem about a Texas sunset and he will. In fact, there's not much the vibrant executive chef isn't open to—except maybe cooking someplace else.

Stephenson has been with Cool River since its opening in 1998, when this still-happening hotspot broke onto the Dallas dining scene with more than just steaks and seafood with a Southwestern twist. Consistently excellent meals served in an unpretentious yet sophisticated setting are what instantly set the restaurant apart—just as they continue to do so.

Though the food and wine are certainly a draw, the cigar and cognac lounge provides a distinctive respite, while a bustling bar with its handcrafted billiard tables and live entertainment pulls in some of the city's most beautiful people.

What to wear: Cool River is a "feel good" place, where you can indulge your senses. Feel good in what you wear. When it's hot outside, we don't mind if people wear nice shorts. But flip-flops, even though they're now being worn to the White House, are not our style. Bottom line: Come to Cool River looking good.

Cool River
1045 Hidden Ridge
Irving, TX 75038
972-871-8881
www.coolrivercafe.com

ABOVE Del Frisco's Wine Cellar. The ultimate dinner for ten. The cellar is built underground with authentic Old-World charm derived from its stone walls, hand-finished pine floor and inventory of award-winning wines from around the world.

FACING PAGE LEFT The cornerstone of Del Frisco's Double Eagle Steakhouse's award-winning menu is USDA Prime Beef and coldwater Australian Lobster tails.

FACING PAGE RIGHT Del Frisco's offers a bar menu for those on the go, an extensive hand-made martini list, full bar of the finest spirits, award-winning wine list and the most sophisticated cognacs.

DEL FRISCO'S DOUBLE EAGLE STEAK HOUSE DALLAS

Dee Lincoln, co-founder
David F. Holben, executive chef

Award-winning Del Frisco's Double Eagle Steak House in Dallas is the flagship of a proven concept. Prime steaks, cold water Australian Lobster tails, succulent seafood, elegance and "swarm service" have earned Del Frisco's recognition as the national powerhouse of the steakhouse domain.

The Del Frisco's legend began in 1981 in New Orleans. By the late 80s, vivacious Dee Lincoln and her business partner moved to Dallas, where they operated two Del Frisco's upscale restaurants. In 1993, the two restaurants consolidated into one location on Spring Valley Road. During the two years that followed, the restaurant continued to soar in popularity.

In 1995, Lone Star Steakhouse & Saloon bought the concept for a record $23 million. Lincoln and Lone Star CEO Jamie Coulter expanded the upscale concept to major cities including Fort Worth, New York City, Las Vegas, and Denver, with Orlando being a special franchisee. Look for more locations to come.

The concept has won numerous awards, including *Restaurants and Institutions'* Ivy Award (bestowed by peers), the Fine Dining Hall of Fame Award from *Nation's Restaurant News*, numerous *Wine Spectator* awards, the 2006 DiRōNa Award, and praise from Zagat Survey as "best steakhouses."

Dallas Del Frisco's is renowned for its inviting ambiance with dark wood, beautiful mirrors, incredible wall coverings, multiple dining rooms, and marble fireplaces, which come together to deliver a sophisticated and romantic mood. Del Frisco's service has been complimented as "upbeat, professional, gracious and embracing."

Every menu item at Del Frisco's is prepared in-house from scratch. Featured performers include hand-cut-to-order USDA Prime steaks, coldwater Australian Lobster tails, scrumptious fresh daily seafood, homemade soups, salad dressings, sauces, and over-the-top side dishes.

"Though we protect our core menu, we remain on the cutting edge with new creativity, such as our monthly winemaker dinners showcasing our innovative culinary style, bar menus for those on the go, and our consideration to health-conscious customers who desire lighter fare," Lincoln says. "It's all part of how we continue to be ahead of trends while still protecting what brought Del Frisco's to the dance."

Most recipes utilize ingredients you'd find in your grandma's kitchen: pure butter, heavy cream, and simple spices. And Lincoln's Cajun beginning is celebrated in big, bold Creole sauces, such as the spicy rémoulade on huge shrimp platters, and the homemade desserts like the signature six-layer Lemon Doberge cake.

What's more, Lincoln says,"We bake our bread fresh everyday so you can rip or tear it, but you aren't allowed to cut it with a knife. At Del Frisco's, you're at my home and every night we break bread together because life is for living."

What to wear: Attire is business casual—no jacket required.

Q&A

MORE ABOUT DEE ...

What color best describes you and why?
Red, because most people describe me as a firecracker.

My friends will tell you I am ...
Real, gregarious, fun, and generous

What business philosophy have you stuck with for years?
Lead by example.

What is the proudest moment in your professional or private life?
Most people would believe it was the sale of Del Frisco's for a record $23 million, but the truth is the birth of my beautiful daughter Bella.

Del Frisco's Double Eagle Steak House Dallas
5251 Spring Valley Road
Dallas, TX 75254
972-490-9000
www.delfriscos.com

ABOVE Food provides the flash in the crisp, cool interior of George Restaurant.

FACING PAGE LEFT Fluer de sel Tasmanian salmon, beurre blanc, succotash and micro greens is only one of the innovations from Chef George Brown.

FACING PAGE RIGHT Situated in the Park Cities, George is a star in the Dallas dining universe.

GEORGE RESTAURANT

Katie and George Brown, chefs and proprietors

Proprietors Katie and George Brown have created a sophisticated, contemporary atmosphere at George Restaurant paired with a modern American menu that allows for innovation and creativity. "It sounds crazy, but we do what we want. We don't limit ourselves to any particular cuisine or ingredients," George says.

Influenced by what is in season and readily available, George changes the menu at least once a week. "We find it easy to add exciting new items to the menu as seasons change because there is nothing like variety when it comes to food," George says as he prepares fruit crisps for the evening. "For example, the blueberries are really rock'n right now."

Cocktails, like cuisine, are also seasonal and taste best when accompanying certain entrées or desserts. Examples of seasonal drinks include peach Cosmos, French lemonade, cranberry martinis and winter punch with marinated pineapple and cinnamon. However, while flux is part of a seasonal menu, some things are sacred. Take chocolate for instance, or the Kennebec pommes frites with white truffle oil sea salt a customer favorite.

Many people visit a restaurant to order what's on the menu, but customers often come to George with special requests. And when those special requests come in, George usually delivers. "I received a call one afternoon from a guy who was

coming in for dinner, and he told me he'd really love some gazpacho. It just so happens that we frequently have these incredible heirloom tomatoes on hand. And, voila we prepared a really nice cold soup for him."

Before chefs Katie and George Brown had their triplets, life was orderly. Take a look at George, a serene room dressed in white tablecloths, white walls and white leather booths. "I'm clean and organized, and I like things a certain way," says George, who opened the restaurant one month before his triplets arrived. "I don't know what I'm going to do with the triplets, because they don't obey the rules of organization," he says with a laugh.

George makes baby food from scratch by the gallons, and in turn, William, Oliver and Clementine have taught him to loosen up. "Now when (purveyor) Tom Spicer shows up at the kitchen back door at 3 in the afternoon and says 'look at these great peaches' and they aren't even on the menu, I say 'cool, come on in, and we'll do a special with it.' It's like having children, you just have to roll with it."

What to wear: Color, definitely. The room is all white, so you're pretty safe wearing color. We have had some people dress in just about everything. I've even thought about adding a No Shorts rule. We also had a guy wearing a cowboy hat in the dining room, and we thought we might have to lasso him!

George Restaurant
George and Katie Brown
7709 Inwood Road
Dallas, TX 75209
214-366-9100
www.georgerestaurant.com

LEFT The Lafayette Room is adorned with hand painted ceilings, a grand fireplace and handmade chandeliers.

RIGHT The Captain's Room is a boardroom style private dining room surrounded with exquisite paintings and varieties of fine wine.

III FORKS

Chris Vogeli, proprietor and executive chef

It took eleven months to build III Forks. Proprietor and executive chef Chris Vogeli was just 33 at the time. That was seven years ago, and the 40-year-old has noticed a few grays, but his enthusiasm for putting great steaks on the table hasn't paled.

Raised in a food-centric family—his father was a chef at the City Club; his aunt and uncle owned a restaurant in Fort Worth—Vogeli learned his culinary skills from his mother. "Mostly because I was hungry and wanted dinner on the table faster," he says, adding that his intent out of college was to make a mint in the computer industry.

Instead, he found his place in the kitchen and now runs a quintessential Dallas steakhouse best known for its 24-karat gold-leaf dome, exquisite steaks and seafood, an uber-extensive wine collection, and near-telepathic service. "Plates come back almost licked clean," Vogeli says. "There's no better compliment than that."

What to wear: Casual business attire.

III Forks
17776 Dallas Parkway
Dallas, Texas 75287
972-267-1776
www.IIIforks.com

ABOVE Main dining room - 13 tables, red, gold, Italian chandelier, romantic.

RIGHT Owner Phil Ramano

IL MULINO

Joe Palladino, managing partner
Philip Romano, owner

It was only natural that Philip Romano would bring Il Mulino to Dallas. A second generation Italian-American from New York, Romano knows good Italian cooking. So does Zagat, the restaurant bible, which regularly ranks Il Mulino the number one Italian restaurant in New York. Romano hired Chef Michael Abruzese, a veteran of Il Mulino New York, to run the kitchen in Dallas as executive chef. He employed a young, fresh staff, including a handpicked maître d', and moved them to New York for a year to train. Romano's efforts have created one of the top restaurants in the country. "We have the best Italian food in the city, bar none. This is the real McCoy," says Romano, who has traveled extensively to Italy with his family and Il Mulino Chief Operating Officer Joe Palladino, to learn about Italian cuisine.

Il Mulino Dallas' sauces are made fresh each day
along with its handmade pastas, and many
ingredients are imported from Italy, such as
buffalo mozzarella and Parmesan cheese. All
wines, including inexpensive ones, are decanted
at the table into crystal pitchers, and dishes such
as zabaglione, a custard flavored with marsala,
are prepared elegantly at tableside in shiny
copper cookware. Chef Abruzese's specialties
include ravioli with black truffle champagne
sauce, rack of lamb, and an array of fresh fish
such as Dover sole, pink snapper, orata, and
branzino. "The veal Milanese is the best I've
ever had," says Romano. "That's my test dish.
If a restaurant does it well, they know what
they're doing."

What to wear: Get excited about the dining
experience and let that determine what you wear.

LEFT Italian paintings, Italian food and pastas.

ABOVE Medici after enjoying a dining experience, head to this semi private club for a high-end, sexy,
exclusive, uptown feeling.

ABOVE Leather VIP booths, dark walnut walls throughout, elevator access and red velvet drapes.

FACING PAGE A collection of 78 pieces of Helmut Newton's black and white nude photography.

Q&A
MORE ABOUT PHILIP ...

Who has made the biggest influence on your career?
My father, Sam, whom my son is named after.

What is something people don't know about you?
I've always been self-employed, since age 16.

What separates you from your competition?
I always strive for uniqueness and originality for each concept I create.

How did you get started in the restaurant business?
My parents were born in Italy. Everything was all about food—so naturally this was the industry I was drawn to.

Il Mulino
2408 Cedar Springs Road
Dallas, TX 75201
214-855-5511
www.ilmulinodallas.com

ABOVE Main dining room.

RIGHT Crispy parmesan cheese basket stuffed with organic greens drizzled with an aged balsamic vinaigrette placed on a bed of vne ripened tomatoes.

Il Sole Restaurant and Wine Bar

Brian and Sonia Black, owners

"Il Sole was five years in the making," says owner Brian Black, who opened Il Sole with wife Sonia in 1999. "Sonia and I wanted to make it our favorite restaurant to go to. It would be warm and quaint with lots of candlelight. Each night at Il Sole we light more than 300 votives." Located above the shops and restaurants at Travis Walk, Il Sole has the ambiance of the wine regions of Tuscany, Provence, and California. Located on the second level, Il Sole's lovely patio has a special view of Knox Henderson's bustling shopping and dining energy below. In the summers, special misters cool the patio 20 degrees below outside temperatures.

While the Blacks' other restaurant, Mi Piaci in Addison, remains true to authentic Italian cuisine, Il Sole's menu is a sophisticated blend of many different cultures. "We serve what I call innovative Italian cuisine, with wines from around the world," says Brian. "I'd be in Napa, or Spain, or Italy, or France, and would taste things that I'd like to incorporate in our menu. We brought lots of ideas back."

Chef Matt Bodnar's innovative food combinations include tender calamari steaks battered in Moretti beer, flash fried, and served with an Oriental

ABOVE Terrace picture looking into the restaurant.

RIGHT Grilled Sea Scallops with a pancetta and sundried tomato risotto cake, micro green salad, apricot butter sauce and crispy capers.

chile sauce; and marinated yellowfin tuna served rare with wasabi mashed potatoes, Asian salad and a sweet soy sauce.

Bread, pasta and pizzas are made fresh daily. The award-winning risotto is made to order, in the traditional Italian method, by stirring it slowly in copper pots until it's rich and creamy. Some of the most popular dishes include penne pasta with vodka tomato sauce, pancetta and crushed red pepper; Italian mushroom ravioli tossed with fresh tomatoes, broccoli, asparagus and fresh herbs; risotto with wild

mushrooms, grated truffles and fresh herbs; and risotto with scallops, mussels, jumbo shrimp, and spicy marinara.

The Big Night menu is an homage to the famous art flick by Stanley Tucci. It's a four-course menu, with four wines paired per course. "We believe that dining is more than a meal," says Brian. "It's an epiphany, an awakening of the senses." If you've ever seen the movie, "Big Night," you understand what he means.

At Il Sole, the Blacks have trained their waitstaff to be true sommeliers who know the restaurant's wine list intimately by region. The wine room, which doubles as a private dining room, contains a collection of more than 3,000 bottles of wine. "We have made sure that everyone walking our floor at Il Sole has a passion for wine," says Brian, whose own passion for wines and Italian cuisine was ignited at 18 years old, during a family trip to Italy. Says Brian: "It didn't take long. We were visiting Monsanto, an 800yearold castle vineyard. That's when I got it. There is so much history, culture and pride that goes into producing a bottle of wine." The Blacks were presented with the *Wine Spectactor* Award of Excellence for their wine list in both 2000 and 2001. Mi Piaci has also won numerous *Wine Specator* Awards, making the Blacks the youngest restaurateurs in Dallas to win the recognition multiple times.

What to wear: Chic casual, jeans are acceptable.

TOP LEFT Cracked black pepper encrusted Atlantic Salmon with carmelized onion whipped potatoes, pomegranate port wine reduction.

TOP RIGHT Winding staircase to the entrance of Il Sole.

RIGHT Bisrto area..

MORE ABOUT BRIAN ...

Name one thing most people don't know about you:
I am a good fisherman.

What CD is in your car right now?
Black Crowes, Live in Las Vegas, 1996.

What is the best part about being a restaurateur?
I get to do something I am passionate about for a living.

What is the highest compliment you've received professionally?
Any time customers tell us Il Sole is their favorite restaurant.

What is the single thing you would do to bring to life a dull meal cooked at home?
Light lots of candles!

What separates you from the competition?
Our ability to outwork our competition.

What do you like most about doing business in Texas?
The people.

Il Sole Restaurant and Wine Bar
4514 Travis St., Suite 201
Dallas, TX 75205
214-559-3888
www.ilsole-dallas.com
events@ilsole-dallas.com

ABOVE Soft lighting and original art in the dining room at Iris creates a warm and comfortable atmosphere. Susie Priore donates the use of the entire restaurant monthly to local fundraisers.

RIGHT The bar at Iris is a neighborhood favorite with the full menu available all night. Local artist Bill Komodore's "Sun Be Silent and Stand Still" makes a fabulous focal point.

IRIS

Susie Priore, owner
Russell Hodges, executive chef

Iris is the quintessential neighborhood restaurant. Nestled in the Inwood Village area of Dallas and surrounded by some of the most sophisticated dining demographics a restaurateur could ever hope for, owner Susie Priore's restaurant is exactly what she wanted: a place that hits on all cylinders food, ambiance, comfort and affordability. When Priore got back from graduate school three years ago, she needed a job. She immediately called longtime friend and chef, Russell Hodges, they teamed up to create the perfect hangout.

Casually elegant might best describe the interior with earth tones and natural materials giving Iris a warmth and lightness. The walls are covered with original art donated to Priore by friends who just happened to be prominent Texas artists; all based on the name of her beloved basenji, Iris.

Russell Hodges, a renowned chef in his own right, brings to the table a talent hard to find these days. His New American cuisine changes seasonally and features only the freshest ingredients. Desserts are all made inhouse, many by Priore herself. The constantly changing wine list features more than 75 percent of its offerings by the glass. It's hard to go wrong with the nightly specials, or the regular menu. Iris truly has something for everyone.

What to wear: Please have on something unless, of course, you have a great body, then suit yourself.

Iris
5405 West Lovers Lane
Dallas, TX 75209
214-352-2727
www.irisdallas.net

ABOVE Whimsically interpreting a casual Texas indoor/outdoor space, Jasper's dining room displays green concrete tabletops with custom lights that were inspired by lanterns on a string.

RIGHT Etched glass embedded with enlarged images of grass form the walls of the board room.

FAR RIGHT Jasper's has a regional sense of place.

JASPER'S

Kent Rathbun, executive chef and proprietor

Executive chef and owner Kent Rathbun calls the food at Jasper's "Gourmet Backyard Cuisine," something over which he's taken a lot of good-natured ribbing. "Who's backyard? Not in my backyard," patrons often say. With an earnest chuckle, Rathbun explains, "This is the type of food you'd get at my house if I were cooking."

With stained concrete floors, teak outdoor-style furniture, bamboo planters, dramatic lighting and artistic interpretations of natural elements, Jasper's is elegant but casual, offering a four-star level of food and service without the fuss of formality, or the four-star price tag. Come by wearing jeans and a tee and start your meal off with the Maytag blue cheese potato chips

followed by the Texas peach barbecued pork loin and finish with the Jasper's signature cherry limeade pie. "It won't take you two hours and you won't spend a bundle but you'll definitely want to spend more time in the backyard," Rathbun says.

For special events and business functions, Jasper's offers a board room, private dining room and off-site catering.

What to wear: "Come as you are," Rathbun says. Shorts during the day are no problem, and jeans are perfectly fine anytime.

Jasper's
The Shops at Legacy
7161 Bishop Road, Suite G-1
Plano, TX 75024
469-229-9111

Jasper's
Market Street: The Woodlands
9595 Six Pines Drive, Suite 900
The Woodlands, TX 77380
281-298-6600

www.jaspers-restaurant.com

ABOVE Dining Room - Reflects old world ambiance - animals on wall are personal trophies.

RIGHT Voted #1 margarita in Dallas - extensive tequila collection keeps crowds coming for 28 years.

JAVIER'S

Javier Gutierrez, proprietor

Tucked into a shady spot on the cusp of Uptown and Highland Park, Javier's is a must that's easy to miss. Still sitting on its original nearly hidden lot, little has changed about the restaurant in nearly 30 years, and owner Javier Gutierrez is happy to maintain the status quo.

His motivation for opening Javier's in 1977 was the absence of real Mexico City cuisine in Dallas at that time. Javier's was a welcome addition to the dining landscape, and it has a formula that continues to work. Yes, small changes have happened a sultry cigar bar was added in 96 and just recently a small patio sprung to life otherwise, the authentic atmosphere and genuine Continental Mexico City menu have stayed very much the same.

Executive chef Juan Reyes, who helped create that menu all those years ago, has been equally dependable. His black bean soup, filet stuffed with cheese, and shrimp in diablo sauce flavored with coffee and orange juice are legendary. There's not a taco or a quesadilla in sight.

But customers? There's no shortage of customers. Javier's is busy every night. And those in the know don't show without a reservation.

What to wear: Customers don't show up looking less than sharp. "We try to maintain a certain level of sophistication, so our dress standards are strict,' Gutierrez says. "People tend to get carried away when you say 'casual.' If you wouldn't wear it to the office, you shouldn't wear it here."

Javier's
4912 Cole Avenue
Dallas, TX 75205
214-521-4211
www.javiers.net

ABOVE The Main Dining Room - lighting, Columbian roses make it cozy and tasteful.

RIGHT Duni pleasures - wine, cakes and flowers.

LA DUNI RESTAURANTS

Espartaco "Taco" Borga, owner
Dunia Borga, pastry chef

La Duni restaurants are a family affair. Espartaco "Taco" Borga runs the business side of La Duni, while his wife, Duni (for whom the restaurants were named) does the baking. Their young son, they like to say, "was born on a flour sack" in the kitchen. "This is a family enterprise," says Taco. "When we opened our first restaurant five years ago on McKinney Avenue we had to bring him with us. Customers would hold him, and sometimes they'd watch him for us. They've seen him grow up."

La Duni on McKinney Avenue, and its newest location on Oak Lawn Avenue share similar menus with a focus on authentic contemporary Latin food. "We are not Latin fusion or Mexican. At La Duni, we bring the foods we were born with to Dallas," says Taco. Known for its handmade sauces

and salsas, specialty desserts, rich coffees, Latin American cocktails, and pan-seared steaks and fish, La Duni is a gourmet restaurant with a friendly neighborhood ambiance.

Weekend brunch is popular among the regulars who frequent La Duni. Favorites are the legendary pastries that Duni Borga makes fresh each morning, such as guava and cheese Glorias, popovers, orange brioche, and mantecadas. There's also a pecan sticky roll, vanilla batter dipped French toast, topped with warm maple-cacique rum-pecan syrup. Or the migas cuatro quesos, with gruyere cheese, provolone, cheddar, and stone ground tortilla chips topped with queso fresco and salsa.

TOP LEFT Best chocolate cake in Dallas, made by Duni.

TOP RIGHT Mojito, award winning.

BOTTOM LEFT One of 22 coffee drinks at La Duni.

BOTTOM RIGHT Breakfast pastries - "Cacao mantecada."

For lunch, there's sandwiches made from freshly baked breads and home roasted meats, such as a citrus marinated pork loin served inside a warm popover. Salads include grilled picanha beef loin medallions on a bed of watercress, spinach, red leaf, cheese arepita, onions, and tomatoes.

Dinner specials include empanadas criollas appetizers, which are crispy white corn masa turnovers filled with Latin cheeses. Favorite entrées are a roasted fish of the day served with mojo de Ajo, Basmati white rice and plantains; flautas filled with hand pulled roasted chicken, tossed with cilantro and tomatoes; and a hand pulled flank steak, stewed in salsa, grilled, and served with Pampero black beans, plaintains, queso fresco and arepas.

ABOVE Patio - refreshing sunny uplifting—perfect for a mojito or a romantic night.

La Duni's waitstaff, bartenders and managers are all of Latin American origin, and the music is equally as authentic. But if you ask Taco Borga the secret to his restaurant's success, he'll tell you it's his wife. "She's who has made us famous."

What to wear: "Wear something that makes you happy," says Taco Borga.

FACING PAGE TOP Oak Lawn location main dining room and coffee bar.

FACING PAGE BOTTOM World famous and most frequently ordered Tres Leche Cake.

ABOVE Oak Lawn coffee studio. Perfect for early morning business breakfast meetings or late night desserts.

MORE FROM TACO...

Name one thing people don't know about you.

I had an acting career that ended when I was seven, and my father, who is also named espartco, is a famous actor in Spain.

If you could eliminate or change one culinary technique, what would it be?

Steaming. I can never get any flavor out of it.

What is the most disastrous project you've ever worked on?

My very first restaurant, in Los Angeles. Anything that could go wrong did.

La Duni Latin Kitchen & Baking Studio
4264 Oak Lawn Avenue
Dallas, TX 75219
214-520-6888

La Duni Latin Café
4620 McKinney Avenue
Dallas, TX 75205
214–520-7300
www.laduni.com

LEFT The Dining Room reflects a casual yet elegant décor reminiscent of Provence.

RIGHT Chef Jean-Marie Cadot and proprietor Pascal Cayet welcome you to Lavendou's terrace decorated with flowers and a Provençal fountain.

LAVENDOU BISTRO PROVENÇAL

Pascal Cayet, proprietor

In the South of France, where Pascal Cayet grew up, people are relaxed. "It's a beautiful life," he says. "No hurry and no worry." Today, however, shuttling between his McKinney Avenue and far North Dallas restaurants, negotiating traffic, and talking on his cell phone, Cayet is anything but worry-free. He's spent the morning at Chez Gérard and is headed north to Lavendou, where he will welcome guests who've come to unwind with a fine bottle of wine and a nice meal.

Chef Jean-Marie Cadot has been in the kitchen at Lavendou from the day it opened in 1996. His sea scallops with leeks and truffles, roasted duck with cassis sauce, and specialty soufflés (raspberry, chocolate, grand marnier) are authentic regional favorites and menu staples at the charming little bistro. The cozy, blue and yellow interior is warm and welcoming. The lattice-covered patio sparkles with white lights in the evening. It's like a sweet retreat to the enchantment and elegant simplicity of Cayet's homeland.

What to wear: It's casual to dressy, but don't stress about it. Just be comfortable.

Lavendou Bistro Provençal
19009 Preston Road, Suite 200
Dallas, TX 75252
972-248-1911
www.lavendou.com

ABOVE The "John Gotti" table seats up to 12—perfect for parties—closes off with dramatic curtains.

RIGHT Foi Gras, one of The Mercury's specialties.

FAR RIGHT Chris Ward.

THE MERCURY GRILL

Chris Ward, executive chef and partner

Speak the name "Chris Ward" and crisped foie gras, rich Roquefort salad dressing, wild mushroom risotto, and pepper-crusted tuna come to mind: every bite impeccably seasoned, every dish flawlessly presented, every meal a miracle. And the miracle worker? A 6-foot–four-inch culinary genius with salt-and-pepper hair and a passion for the finest foods on earth.

Chris Ward, executive chef and partner in Restaurant Life, the fine dining division of MCrowd Restaurant Group, has become synonymous with the restaurants he's helped create—and none more so than his first, the jewel that is The Mercury Grill. "The food is a reflection of me and my tastes. Our

menu reflects my moods on what I like to eat," he says.

Named Restaurant of the Year by *The Dallas Morning News* when it opened in 1998, The Mercury has demonstrated a steadfast commitment to high standards and uncompromised quality. And the self-described workaholic, who, after 25 years in the restaurant business, is still in the kitchen every night until 10, works closely with his chefs to ensure that they convey that imperative with precision, that every plate that leaves their hands is exactly as if he prepared it himself.

As unwavering dedication to one's craft often does, Ward's single-

RIGHT Sleek clean lines - timeless
style/decor is tailored.

mindedness has paid off immeasurably. At 46 years old, he's not only a successful restaurateur with nearly every industry accolade to his credit, he's a celebrity chef who's been called upon to cook for the president of the United States. "There's only one word to describe it: surreal. I'd never even been to Washington, D.C., and when I walked up the White House steps, my heart was going pitter-patter." That excitement paled in comparison to what he felt later, when a server signaled him and said, "The president wants to see you." Yet nothing in his career tops the moment when President George W. Bush told him "Dinner was fabulous."

Leader of the free world and first lady aside, Ward is, more often than not,

cooking for mere mortals, serving signature dishes, like pearl couscous with carbonara and a poached egg, and nightly specials in an understated environment. "The Mercury is a neighborhood restaurant with national acclaim," he says. That means a clientele of foodies from far and wide as well as regulars who dine there two or three times a week. They go seeking the extraordinary—and they get it.

What to wear: Something casual but nice. People don't really wear jeans but most don't wear suits, either.

FACING PAGE "113" is a bar with semi-private dining - a lounge off the main dining - plush decor.

RIGHT Tufted wall with abstract art - private table set with minimalistic white china and fine crystal stemware.

MORE ABOUT CHRIS ...

What's it like to go to a dinner party at your house?
Almost all the time we go around the table and name what famous people, living or dead, we'd like to join us. Even before I was asked to cook for him, I'd say George W. Bush, Ronald Reagan, Jack Nicklaus, Jack Nicholson, and Jacqueline Bissett. This livens things up, gets people talking, and makes people think.

What is your favorite food?
I can eat foie gras anytime, anyplace. I've been cooking it for a long time and am happy to see its renewed popularity on restaurant menus.

What color best describes you?
Orange is my favorite color, always has been. It's flashy and different. Plus, I was born on Halloween.

If you weren't a chef, what would you be doing?
Piloting a commercial aircraft.

What personal indulgence do you spend the most money on?
Custom suits from Chris Despos and shoes.

The Mercury Grill
11909 Preston Road
Dallas, TX 75230
972-960-7988
www.mcrowd.com

LEFT The Mercy Bar is scalloped in shape.

RIGHT Hours of operation.

MERCY WINE BAR

Glen Agritelley, proprietor

Glen Agritelley is Roy Orbison's biggest fan. Not only does he have the largest private collection in the United States of the late singer's memorabilia, but the name of his two-year-old wine bar, Mercy, was inspired by Orbison's lyrics. The second line of the famous song, "oh, Pretty Woman," goes like this: No one could look as good as you...mercy! "I've got everything belonging to Orbison from his 1985 Porsche Cabriolet to signed contracts and his stage clothes," says Agritelley, a successful entrepreneur who owns private sports club TbarM Racquet Club, and men's clothing store Sebastian's Closet. He learned each business from

the ground up, and he believes that it was this fresh point of view that made the ventures successful. "My three businesses all revolve around lifestyle," he says. "Providing products and service to higher-end clients are what it's all about."

Agritelley is not your average businessman, and Mercy is not your average restaurant. Wine is served from crystal carafes and in crystal glasses. Most of the 50 wines by the bottle and 100 wines by the glass are unique to Mercy you won't find them in liquor stores and many restaurants don't

LEFT Glen's Lamborghini in front of Mercy on a balmy night.

RIGHT Dining area from the Mezzanine.

make them available by the glass. "I wanted people to try great wines, but while they might not buy a $200 bottle of fine wine, they'll pay $20 or $30 to try a glass of it."

Mercy's sommelier and manager is 26-year-old France born Vincent Havard, a graduate of Lycée Hotelier in France who has worked in the hospitality business all over the world. Havard tastes and selects new wines each day to keep the menu fresh and unexpected. Unlike most restaurants which pair wines to food, Mercy does the opposite, pairing food to wine. "We are all about wine," says Agritelley. "We help our guests choose their wines first based on what they like, then we suggest dishes that will go well with it."

Schylur Snowden, Mercy's 23-year-old up and coming chef, has created a European style menu to pair beautifully with the restaurant's broad list of wines, champagnes and beers. Portions are small but intensely flavorful, and many dishes are designed to be shared, such as crab cakes with citrus aioli, herbed goat cheese served warm with crostinis, and the killer pommes frites.

Paella is served every Friday and Saturday night, and paired with a good Spanish wine. The menu is changed twice a year, but seasonal specials, including fish, are offered regularly.

The staff at Mercy is young but well-trained. "I just came back from taking the whole staff to Napa Valley," says Agritelley, who believes in empowering employees with knowledge and enthusiasm, then getting out of the way and letting them do their jobs. "They get excited about what they experience and bring that energy to the table," he says.

Mercy's decor is everything you want a wine bar to be intimate, sexy, and sophisticated. Inspired by clubs and restaurants in Miami, Los Angeles, New York, and Italy, Mercy has an ergonomical y correct, serpentine marble bar like one Agritelley saw in Nashville, which allows people to see others at the bar without straining. Thin, linen sheers separating the lounge and restaurant areas were inspired by the Delano Hotel in Miami, while the hand painted murals were envisioned after a trip to Venice and Pompeii.

"We want to make the experience of coming to Mercy more than just dining out," says Agritelley. "We want it to be the best part of their day."

What to wear: "Drinking shirts! They are fun, going-out shirts for men in bold colors and stripes and paisleys. Men wear them with shirttails out. We see everything from beat up jeans to suits and ties. It's a very European feel. The women get dressed up."

FACING PAGE LEFT Draped lounge for very private parties.

ABOVE Glen enjoying a glass of vino.

ABOVE Clean lines, colorful art, graphic architecture are what our customers relate to.

RIGHT Form, function, stylish.

MI COCINA

Mico Rodriquez, proprietor

In 1991, at the age of 34, Mico Rodriguez was about to open his first restaurant. He had spent a lifetime working in the restaurant business. When he was just 6 years old, he started helping his parents, who worked for El Chico. Later, when they opened the now famous Mia's, in 1982, he was right beside them.

Stepping out on his own, however, was a huge risk. He and his wife, Caroline, backed by three partners, were opening their unique version of a Mexican restaurant in an unproven area of Dallas.

"At the time, restaurant design was all about making things look broken down," Rodriguez recalls. "I moved away from that with clean colors and minimal art. Food-wise, I wanted to raise the bar in terms of quality. That meant fresh chicken—never frozen—and top-quality beef. But we didn't stop there. We looked at the rice, the beans, everything and found ways to ratchet things up."

Dallas diners noticed. People began talking about a little restaurant with only 12 tables that was serving great Mexican food. Nearly 15 years later, though the classic recipes that established the brand remain, Mi Cocina now offers a diverse selection of interior-Mexico food items.

As the menu has grown, so has the company. From that first location, Mi Cocina's has spread to 15 locations across Dallas and Fort Worth as well

as Kansas City and Houston. M Crowd, the parent company, owns and operates a total of 34 restaurants, including Taco Diner, Mainstream Fish House, and The Mercury Grill.

The appeal of Mi Cocina hinges on the food, of course, but the loyalty of the service staff also is a huge reason for its continued prosperity. Nine of the original 12 employees are still with the company., and many of them are now managers. Rodriguez is stubborn about promoting from within, believing that when job openings arise the people already working for the company deserve the chance to advance. "Nurturing a family atmosphere is essential to our success," Rodriguez notes.

Customers are loyal, too. "One customer, in fact, said, 'Mico, your restaurants are the way I want to live my life.' That's the biggest compliment anyone has ever given me." Rodriguez says. "Good taste, good manner, and integrity—that's what we are all about. We don't try to be cute. We don't pretend we're in Mexico. This is your neighborhood Mexican restaurant, circa 2010."

What to wear: "Ours is a casual restaurant, but people walk straight out of Chanel or Hermés and into dinner," Rodriguez says.

ABOVE "See you in the restaurants," Mico and family.

ABOVE RIGHT "Art is an expression of our culture."

FACING PAGE The "Third Floor"....Dallas' best kept secret.

MORE ABOUT MICO ...

What do you do to bring life to a dull meal cooked at home?
Surround myself with people who are entertaining. Even the best meal isn't as exciting as a group of colorful people.

What is the most unique/impressive/beautiful restaurant in which you've dined in Texas?
The French Room, because you are transcended into another world, and Nana, because I can sit up in the sky and look at my city.

My friends will tell you I am ...
Very generous.

What color best describes you and why?
Red, because I am so passionate about my restaurants.

Mi Cocina
77 Highland Park Village
Dallas, TX 75205
214-521-4626
www.mcrowd.com

ABOVE Main Dining Room 2.

RIGHT North Dining Room (Private).

MI PIACI

Brian and Sonia Black, owners

When Mi Piaci opened in 1991, it was hailed as one of the best Italian restaurants in Texas. It still is. Mi Piaci serves Northern Italian cuisine from recipes that are hundreds of years old. "We have stayed true to authentic Italian cuisine," says Brian Black, who along with his wife Sonia, own and operate Mi Piaci in Addison, and Il Sole in Dallas' Uptown area. At Mi Piaci, everything is made fresh each day. "We cure our own meats, make our own pasta, and bake five types of bread daily," says Black. "Our risotto is cooked to order, not in advance. We even grow our own fresh herbs. If we cannot make the product in-house, we will import it from Italy."

Like the Italians, Chef Carlos Fuentez uses simple, high quality ingredients, from the finest olive oils, to the best risottos, and Durham flour. Some of his specialties include osso buco à la Milanese, and braised veal shank. "Our sea bass is lovely," says Black. "It's a favorite customer dish, along with whole Dover sole. We brush it lightly in olive oil, then grill it. It's deboned table side, with a little lemon squeezed on top. It's to die for."

One of the most acclaimed dishes is the saffron risotto. "I'm very proud of our risottos," says Black. "*Texas Monthly* wrote that ours are the best in

Texas. We cook our risottos the traditional Italian way, slowly for 30 minutes in copper pots. Our chefs stand over the hot stove and stir and stir without stopping until it's a perfect, creamy consistency." Mi Piaci has received accolades for its cuisine from Zagat, *Gourmet*, *Food & Wine*, *Esquire*, *Town & Country*, *Restaurant Hospitality*, *Wine Enthusiast Magazine* and *Best Restaurants in America Magazine*.

Mi Piaci has one of the state's only all-Italian wine lists, serving the finest Chianti, Barolo, Piedmont, and Pino Grigio wines, among others. Wines are offered by the bottle and by the glass. "People didn't know what Italian wine was in the 90s when we opened," says Black. That has since changed. "Our wine list just won its 10th award of excellence in the respected *Wine Spectator* magazine.

Mi Piaci's stunning interiors were designed by renowned designer Emily Summers, who provided a soft, comfortable look, evocative of a sophisticated country home in Tuscany. There are three dining rooms and two private rooms, including the Map Room, with a 30-foot vaulted ceiling. A wine cellar holds up to 26 people, and is a popular room for small dinners and wine tastings. For an easy, relaxed dinner, try the bar, which serves a full menu.

LEFT Antipasta Station.

ABOVE Wine Cellar (Private).

Lots of natural light from two big skylights wash over the restaurant's polished hardwood floors and make the crystal sparkle. Large windows in the back and the outdoor patio offer a view of a shimmering, private lake with ducks. "In a time where people are designing restaurants with a slick, colder feel, our design will always be a place that, after a hard day, people feel like they can relax," says Black.

What to wear: Sophisticated elegance.

Q&A

MORE ABOUT
BRIAN ...

What personal indulgence do you spend the most money on?

My wife and children.

The one thing people don't know about you?

I'd rather be fishing.

What is the best part of being a restaurateur?

I am able to share memorable experiences with our customers, such as birthdays, engagements, and anniversaries.

Who has made the biggest impact on your career?

The customer. They continue to surprise us and cheer us on.

What is the single thing you would do to bring to life a dull meal cooked at home?

Season the food properly.

Mi Piaci
14854 Montfort Drive
Dallas, TX 75240
972-934-8424
www.mipiaci-dallas.com

ABOVE Guests enjoy a pre-dinner cocktail in the bar.

FACING PAGE LEFT Naan's lounge draws a hip crowd.

FACING PAGE RIGHT Naan's well-appointed dining room has a sophisticated vibe.

NAAN

Sasha Kim, owner and proprietor

Sasha Kim gave Dallas its first-ever modern Korean restaurant in 2003. Sleek and sophisticated, with a young, trendy vibe, Naan delivers traditional Korean food and sushi in an atmosphere that is as cosmopolitan as the city that surrounds it. The restaurant takes its name from the Korean word for orchid; through the subtle placement of the exotic flower throughout, the name resonates. "Naan is a place where you can come in, eat great food, enjoy a cocktail in the lounge and hang out with your friends," Kim says.

At 31, Sasha is unlike the typical Korean restaurant owner. She is the daughter of successful restaurateur Sung Hui Kim, who owns Dallas' popular Korea House Restaurant. Sasha was born in New York and educated at Sotheby's Institute of Art and the American University in London where she earned a master's degree in art history.

Inspired by her mother and influenced by her time abroad, Sasha recognized a gap in the Dallas dining scene. She filled it with a restaurant both refined and forward-thinking, with a luxe, contemporary decor. And the food? According to one local dining critic, "it'll rock your world."

What to wear: Something hip and fun. Our guests make an effort to get dressed up.

Naan
The Shops at Legacy
7161 Bishop Road
Plano, TX 75024
972-943-9288
www.naanrestaurant.com

LEFT A panoramic view of the Dallas skyline awaits guests at Nana.

RIGHT Elegant private dining with Versace china.

NANA

Paul Pinnell, general manager
Anthony C. Bombaci, executive chef

"The best restaurant in Dallas isn't in Dallas, it's above it!"

Nana's highly acclaimed food, service, and decor draw crowds nightly to the 27th floor of the Dallas landmark Anatole Hotel. Boasting an award-winning panoramic view of downtown, the restaurant's critically acclaimed cuisine, service and premier wine cellar is dramatically enhanced by an elegant interior, including a priceless collection of Asian art from the private collection of Margaret and Trammell Crow.

Nana's newly energized and remodeled space offers an array of museum-quality artwork. Magnificently carved jade horses and a reclining gold Buddha greet guests in the foyer, an artistic preface to an evening of distinction. This glimpse of Nana prepares one for the breathtaking aesthetics and unforgettable cuisine of the restaurant itself.

Nana General Manager, Paul Pinnell, deftly directs seasoned service staff to ensure a memorable dining experience. Known as the "Dean of Dallas Maître d's," Pinnell's pays attention to every detail, securing Nana's stellar reputation as offering the finest in attentive service.

TOP LEFT Three Spoons representing the Triangle Flavor Philosophy.

TOP RIGHT Ahi Tuna tartar with wasabi sorbet, passion fruit and soy-sesame coulis.

BOTTOM LEFT Crispy Skinned Suckling Pig with Mango "noodles" and Cilantro.

BOTTOM RIGHT Nana dinner menu with award-winning wine.

Wine director Rudy Mikula transcends traditional wine service as he expertly oversees an impeccably stocked cellar that has garnered national fame.

World renowned executive chef Anthony C. Bombaci presides over the kitchen, using only the finest products available in local, national, and international markets, to create simple, precise and recognizable food that is seasoned and cooked to perfection. Combining creative American cuisine with modern European influences, Bombaci's menu offers brilliant flavors from the Catalan, Spanish, and Italian regions. Inventive new menu items include Pine Island oysters with celery root puree and green apple sorbet; prosciutto-wrapped chicken breast with upside-down Parmigiano rice pudding; and seared shrimp with Pedro Jimenez nectar.

Bombaci's cuisine quickly became a trend in Dallas when he took over the Nana helm in 2005 and received "Five-Stars" for cuisine from *The Dallas Morning News*.

What other awards has Nana received? Nana is proud to be among a selected group of premier establishments in North America honored with "Four-Stars" from the *Mobil Travel Guide*, "Four-Diamonds" from AAA, 2006 Distinguished Restaurant of North America (DiRōNA) Award recipient and "*Wine Spectator's* Best of Award of Excellence."

What do wear: The dress code is casual elegance.

ABOVE The bar's focal point is a treasure and restaurant namesake: Nana by Artist Gospodin Suchorowsky.

BELOW Nana Executive Chef Anthony C. Bombaci.

Q&A

MORE ABOUT TONY ...

What is Chef Bombaci's philosophy in the Nana kitchen?
Chef Bombaci uses the Triangle Food Philosophy which is based on putiry and respect for principle of product, including the highest of quality–and garnished with interesting flavors, marriages and contrasts. The three cornerstone of the triangle refer to the heart, the hands, and the mind. The simplest food...is the hardest to execute perfectly!

What else should people know about Nana?
In addition to the 170-seat dining room, Nana accommodates larger parties with the same five-star cuisine and view in one of five well-appointed private dining suites. Also, considered the "hot-spot" for jazz and dancing, the stunningly renovated Bar at Nana features an enlarged dance floor with a centrally located band stand, reinforcing Nana's commitment to the finest in live music entertainment nightly. Complimentary valet parking is available for guests' convenience.

Nana
Anatole Hotel
2201 Stemmons Freeway, 27th Floor
Dallas, TX 75207
214-761-7470
www.nanarestaurant.com

NEWPORT'S SEAFOOD & STEAKS

Steven Laham, owner and operator

As a college graduate, Steven Laham came to Dallas from Kansas to work at the Four Seasons Resort and Club in Las Colinas. Before long he was applying what he learned there to his own award-winning establishment. At just 29 years old, Laham purchased the well-established Newport's, already famous for fresh seafood and a lively fine-dining atmosphere.

Though the restaurant changed hands, the impeccable food and service remained the same under its new owner, as did the chef. Salvador Soto has been at Newport's since it opened in 1983. Only a teenager his first day on the job, the executive chef practically grew up in the kitchen. Today he turns out original, made-from-scratch sauces and consistently superb and imaginative entrées like a coconut-crusted salmon over a kicky mango

relish made with jalapeno peppers or a delish ginger-plum barbecued swordfish with vegetables roasted over mesquite wood flames. And his Key lime pie? "People go nuts over it," Laham says.

What to wear: During the day we draw a downtown business crowd, so you'll see a lot of suits. At night, it's a bit more casual.

LEFT Dim lighting and modern art give Newport's main dining room a sophisticated feel.

TOP RIGHT Newport's Lounge overlooking the dining room.

BOTTOM RIGHT The majestic ship over the wall was originally part of the Seaman's Chapel in Copenhagen.

TOP LEFT Angus beef and jumbo prawns prepared on the mesquite grill.

TOP RIGHT Vanilla bean créme brulé topped with fresh-whipped cream and fresh berries.

BOTTOM LEFT "One of the best in the country," says Delta Sky Magazine of Newport's Key Lime Pie.

BOTTOM RIGHT Fresh Chilean Seabass cooked over mesquite wood grill.

MORE ABOUT STEVEN ...

What's most unusual about Newport's?
The spacious West End restaurant is housed in the pre-Prohibition-era Dallas Brewery and Bottling Works building. Its 31-feet-wide, still-active artesian well remains as the architectural focal point.

What is the best part of being a restaurateur?
I enjoy the guests, taking them to their tables, making them feel special. My favorite part of being an owner is that I can control the work environment. I like to have fun and enjoy my job; therefore, I want the same for my employees. Guests can see whether someone enjoys his job.

Who has had the biggest influence on your career?
My father and brother.

What's one thing most people don't know about you?
I'm from Kansas.

My friends would tell you...
That I am generous.

Newport's Seafood & Steaks
703 McKinney Avenue
Dallas, TX 75202
214-954-0220
www.newports.us

ABOVE Wine room, seats up to 35 people, dark mahogany, private parties and images of California wineries adorn walls.

RIGHT Main dining room seats 200 people. Center table "sterling table" seats up to 14 people–piano player alibaster chandeliers/ amber.

NICK & SAM'S

Joe Paladino, co-owner
Philip Romano, owner

Nick & Sam's is not your run-of-the-mill steak house—they have the largest selection of prime aged beef and the largest selection of fish of any steak house in the country. The kitchen is manned by acclaimed Culinary Institute of America grad Chef Samir Dhurandhar, whose prime aged bone-in tenderloin, Japanese Kobe beef, award-winning Caesar salad, seared Diver scallops, and lemon sole meunière have garnered national critical attention and loyal customers.

Philip Romano, who founded Nick & Sam's, says: "We were the first to create a new look and feel in a steakhouse. When you walk in, you enter through the wine cellar. We have the best wine you can have along with the best food available." Romano has created more than 25 successful national restaurant concepts including Fuddrucker's, Romano's Macaroni Grill, and eatZi's Market & Bakery.

ABOVE Bar area, sophisticated yet warm atmoshere is very popular for happy hour, walnut wood floors and an elegant fire place.

BELOW Long bar with lamp lights is an ideal setting.

A second generation Italian American from New York, Romano hired former New York City cop-turned-Las Vegas restaurateur Joseph Palladino to help open the restaurant. Palladino is co-owner of Nick & Sam's and the managing partner for Il Mulino. "Nick & Sam's is a great value for the guest," says Palladino. "We are the only steakhouse that serves complementary caviar and a complementary glass of port at the end of the meal."

The restaurant boasts more than 700 fine wines, and a wine flight program of 30 wines by the glass, served each evening at the bar. The Ultimate Experience is a special reservation wine flight program that includes complementary caviar, and shellfish appetizers at Nick & Sam's raw bar, paired with wines of your choice.

Some of Chef Dhurandhar's specialties are Coloraco lamb porterhouse, prime aged rib eye, and jumbo lump crab cakes. The raw bar is one of the most popular aspects of Nick & Sam's, where guests can order Beluga, Sevruga, and Osetr caviars, Little Neck clams, and oysters of the day. Some of Nick & Sam's most popular desserts are a chocolate molten soufflé, strawberry cheesecake, banana fritters, and an espresso float.

ABOVE Burgundy room—also used for private parties, seats up to 80 people—also stores 3,000 wines.

The interiors are elegant in dark woods and romantic candlelight, appealing to both women and men, says Romano. Two private wine rooms are available to host dinners and small events. Romano's favorite touch: a grand piano that sits smack in the middle of the open kitchen.

The restaurant biz runs deep in the Romano family's blood. His nine-year-old Sam, for whom the restaurant was named, can be seen many nights dressed in a little Italian suit, handing out menus at the door and showing guests to their tables. "He's growing so fast, we have to buy him a new suit every month," says Romano.

What to wear: "Dress to impress, you'll never know who you might see."

Q&A

MORE ABOUT JOSEPH ...

Who has made the biggest impact on your career?
Phil Romano.

What one element of cooking or business philosophy have you stuck with for years, which still works?
Never compromise the integrity of the food. Customers deserve the best in food and service.

If you could eliminate or change one culinary technique, cuisine or style from the world, what would it be?
I wish there was more awareness of how much effort goes into food preparation.

What personal indulgence do you spend the most money on?
Brioni suits.

A disastrous event?
There was a big convention in town, Dallas had a three-cay ice storm, and I'd just gotten a $25,000 shippment of meat. People couldn't get to the restaurant, so I rented three stretch Hummers and went to the hotels to pick up guests and brought them to Nick & Sam's. We packed them in.

Nick and Sam's
3008 Maple Avenue
Dallas, TX 75201
214-871-7444
www.nick-sams.com

ABOVE The charm and elegance of Old Hickory Steakhouse is discovered as you descend our spiral staircase into a Texas inspired wine-cellar dining room.

RIGHT Fine wines and Artisanal cheeses are showcased at Old Hickory Wine Shoppe.

OLD HICKORY STEAKHOUSE

Tom Fleming, executive chef

Guests dining at Old Hickory Steakhouse, Gaylord Texan Resort are delighted to find a grand spiral staircase leading them down to the old-world charm and warm, rich atmosphere of a Texas wine-cellar. As the signature restaurant of Gaylord Hotels for more than 28 years, Old Hickory Steakhouse is committed to serving the finest steaks and seafood available. The steakhouse also features artisanal cheeses, an extensive wine list, and three private dining rooms.

A crowd-pleaser from the moment the doors first opened, Old Hickory drew quick praise from both local and national food critics as well as local residents and hotel guests. Chef Tom Fleming, a 25-year restaurant veteran who earned a reputation as a culinary standout in the kitchen at Dallas's Riviera anc Lombardi Mare, has assembled a highly skilled culinary team. Already the restaurant has earned several awards, including 2004 Top Ten New Restaurants from The Dallas Morning News and Best Dessert of 2004 from the Dallas Observer. Additionally, the restaurant was met with praise by D Magazine, and Nation's Restaurant News called it a Dallas hot spot.

TOP LEFT Filet of beef with roasted Maine lobster, sauce béarnaise and crisp onions.

TOP RIGHT Tartar of Filet and Carpaccio of New York Strip with white truffle oil and parmesan cheese.

BOTTOM LEFT Key Lime Tart with graham cracker-coconut crust.

BOTTOM RIGHT Chilled Permian Basin Shrimp Salad "Louis Style" with fresh avocado and basil oil.

An expert in the kitchen, Fleming prepares dazzling appetizers like seared foie gras with apple-raisin compote; seafood selections such as sautéed lemon-scented scallops with pearl couscous and thyme-vermouth sauce, and potato-crusted salmon with caramelized red onion-merlot sauce; and, of course, mouthwatering chops and Black Angus steaks, seasoned to perfection with butter, cracked pepper, and kosher salt and grilled to exact specifications. Fleming's extraordinary skill is evident in the inspired desserts not found elsewhere: Tangy lemon cannoli with blueberry and raspberry coulis, apple doughnuts with warm caramel sauce, and bananas Foster with coconut gelato and crispy plantains send even die-hard sweet tooths home happy.

"Fine wine is the beverage of choice for celebrations, and one of our goals at Gaylord Texan is to promote the importance of celebrating life as often as possible," Fleming says. To illustrate that, each year the Wine and Food Society kicks off the New Year with the annual Denim & Diamonds Dinner at Old Hickory Steakhouse, featuring the portfolio of fine wines from Kendall-

ABOVE Guests will enjoy dining "Al Fresco" on our vineyard terrace.

Jackson. The Old Hickory Wine Shoppe, overlooking the resort's vineyard, is a great place to relax. The outdoor, lantern-lit dining area, which features three fireplaces, is perfect for toasting a Texas sunset. And true wine and food enthusiasts might consider joining the Gaylord Texan Wine & Food Society (www.texanwineandfoodsociety.com).

With three distinctive private dining areas, Old Hickory is the perfect place for a private party. The Cellar, in our wine-cellar, seats 10, the unique Barrell Room has seating for 30 and the Bacchus Room overlooking the patio area seats 60. All make for an unforgettable dining experience.

Old Hickory Steakhouse is located in the resort's Lone Star Tower. Complimentary parking is available to all guests dining in the hotel. Enjoy a leisurely stroll through the spectacular Gaylord Resort as a prelude to an incredible meal.

What to wear: Texas comfortable.

RIGHT Chef Tom Fleming.

LEFT Vaulted ceilings, scrolled iron-works and soft-muted colors add character and warmth to our guest's dining experience.

MORE FROM TOM ...

What personal indulgence do you spend the most money on?
Woodworking tools. I build furniture as a hobby.

Whose CD are you listening to in your car right now?
Ray Charles.

What one element of cooking have you stuck with through the years?
Buy only the best available products. Never let price be the determining factor.

Who has had the biggest impact on your career?
My brother, Robert Fleming, a great restaurateur!

What do you like most about doing business in Texas?
Texans are well-traveled and have discriminating palates. They are a pleasure to cook for.

Old Hickory Steakhouse
Gaylord Texan Resort & Convention Center
1501 Gaylord Trail
Grapevine, TX 76051
817-778-1000
www.gaylordhotels.com/gaylordtexan

ABOVE 18 oz. Prime New York Strip dry aged in house.

RIGHT Exterior of Pappas Bros. Steakhouse located at I35 and Northwest Highway in Dallas.

PAPPAS BROS. STEAKHOUSE

Rick Turner, general manager
Norman Reola, executive chef

With so many high-end steakhouses to choose from in the Dallas area, a restaurant needs to be something extra special to stand out. For Pappas Bros. Steakhouse, a big part of what sets it apart from the competition is their beef.

There's really no secret to making a great steak, according to Rick Turner, general manager of Pappas Bros. It's dry-aging—a process that involves painstaking time and expense—that makes a Pappas Bros. steak sublime. Dry-aging is so labor-intensive that most steakhouses don't even bother with it. But Pappas Bros. isn't most steakhouses. It's one of only a handful nationwide that dry-ages its meat on the premises.

"We're passionate about the quality of our food. That's why we're willing to make the significant investment of time and money that few other restaurants are willing to make," Turner says. "We purchase our Prime beef untrimmed and dry-age for 30 to 40 days on racks in a specially-constructed, nearly sterile, temperature- and humidity-controlled room. This process removes moisture from the meat, which intensifies the flavor and brings out the tenderness. It's someone's full-time job to watch and care for that meat. It's a very intensive process, but the results are worth it."

Whether or not a guest immediately recognizes the difference between a cut of meat that's been dry-aged and one that's been "aged" by less expensive methods is immaterial, says Turner. It's part of a learning process

ABOVE Pappas Bros. Steakhouse has over 2,200 different wine selections on our extensive wine list. One of the best wine lists in the state.

RIGHT Culinary–trained chefs put the finishing touches on our delicious dishes.

that makes for loyal customers. Once they eat a steak at Pappas Bros., they won't want a steak from anywhere else.

Dry-aging onsite is just one reason that people keep coming to Pappas. Bros., even in a steakhouse-heavy market like Dallas. "There are two things people come to Pappas Bros. for," Turner says. "The quality of our food and the quality of our service, both of which contribute to a superior dining experience. And we excel in all aspects of food, atmosphere, and service, which are what make a dining experience extra special."

And that experience begins when you enter the 1930s-Chicago-styled steakhouse, founded by Houston's Pappas family, which own and operate

Pappadeaux Seafood Kitchen and Pappasito's Cantina chain, among others. Though these two predecessors are casual restaurants with numerous locations, Pappas Bros. Steakhouse is one of only two in the nation—the other is in Houston—and both are icons worthy of Frank Sinatra, who can be heard crooning softly in the background as guests enjoy their meals.

The menu comprises steak, seafood, and an assortment of delectable, family-style side dishes. Standouts include sensuous turtle gumbo, fresh and succulent bacon-wrapped scallops, thick crab cakes, big-eye pepper-crusted tuna, and, of course, the dry-aged Prime beef—tender filet mignon juicy rib eye, thick New York strip, and perfect porterhouse.

Fine wine is a crucial detail at any high-end steakhouse, and, true to its nature, Pappas Bros. has a wine cellar that's talked about by wine professionals across the country. With more than 2,200 selections of nearly 31,000 bottles handpicked from the finest vineyards, including a $70,000 bottle of 1945 Romanée Conti—one of just two in the world—the collection is among the best in the state. "It's wonderful to work in a place with such a fantastic wine cellar," Turner says. And with four sommeliers on the floor at all times, guests can choose the right wine with confidence every time.

Such is the service across the board. Seasoned servers are prompt, highly attentive, and rigorously trained, as are all the staff, from dishwashers to managers. The produce and seafood are fresh, the cuts of meat incomparable. Even the grade of leather on the booth seats and the carpet on the floor are chosen for their superior quality.

Excellent beef, delicious dishes, superior service and an overflowing wine cellar: It's no secret that Pappas Bros. Steakhouse will be wowing diners for a long time to come.

What to wear: In the course of an evening, you'll see someone wearing a golf shirt and a pair of slacks, and at the next table someone is wearing a tuxedo. We tell our guests that business casual is fine, but we recommend a coat and tie, especially in the evening.

ABOVE Pappas Bros. Steakhouse is the total dining experience: excellent beef, delicious dishes, superior service and an overflowing wine cellar.

Q&A
MORE FROM
RICK . . .

What business philosophy do you abide by?
The finest quality food and the best service. Our guests come back because they know they'll get great food and great service every time.

What color best describes you and why?
Navy blue, because it's strong, steadfast, regal and demands respect.

What surprises guests about the restaurant?
The intense flavor of our beef that we so painstakingly prepare.

What personal indulgence do you spend the most money on?
Personal improvement such as books, education, gym membership and nutritional items.

Pappas Bros. Steakhouse
10477 Lombardy Lane
Dallas, TX 75220
214-366-2000
www.pappasbros.com

ABOVE Barrel Room—hand–troweled Italian plaster with Alabaster chandeliers (main dining).

RIGHT Perry's grand entrance.

PERRY'S RESTAURANT

Amie Bergus, proprietor and owner
Travis Henderson, chef and owner
Bill Esping, partner and owner

Whenever a new restaurant opens, the owners take a risk. And when Amie Bergus and Travis Henderson were in the planning stages for Perry's, they'd considered well what they were getting into. No strangers to the food service industry, the pair have a combined 42 years in the restaurant biz, and though Dallas had plenty of high-end steakhouses, they saw a void and set out to fill it with a more personable approach. What they didn't count on were the events of September 11, 2001.

Less determined partners might have postponed the restaurant's opening, but Bergus and Henderson soldiered on with fortitude and hope in the wake of national disaster. Perry's served dinner for the first time just two months later. "It was our heart and soul, our baby, and we decided to move forward with it," Bergus remembers.

Around the nation and across the board times were tough, and they learned to treat every customer who came through their door like the only one who would ever appear. They built their business one very appreciated guest at a time, learning diners' names, where they like to sit, what they like to drink, when their birthdays and anniversaries fall, and generally investing a lot of emotion in each individual. "Looking back, it really provided us with a huge standard for food and service," Bergus says.

It's a benchmark that quickly won the hearts (and stomachs) of patrons, inspiring an astounding 80 percent of guests to return to Perry's again and again, with many regulars supping there two or more times per week. And it's a measure that Perry's continues to uphold four years later.

ABOVE Secluded high back booth seating.

RIGHT Red curtain booths - (Madia booths). Reserved months in advance.

Situated at the tip of a triangular lot in Uptown (the 76th property Bergus looked at and a spot she says "sung" to her when she saw it), the restaurant has a prime location for its Prime beef and seafood menu and its black-napkin interior design. The atmosphere is plush but not ostentatious and, thanks to Amie's feminine touch, it has a softer feel than most steakhouses. Chocolate brown leather booths; dual-toned, hand-troweled plaster walls; hand-scraped wood floors; and glowing, alabaster lighting, "which makes everyone look pretty," create a warm, comfortable space.

The food is equally exquisite. Henderson is a veteran of Café Pacific and Newport's and he knows seafood. His kitchen delivers dishes like toasted pecan-crusted rainbow trout with orange-rosemary butter sauce–a perennial "special"—and blackened redfish with avocado and char chil-tomato sauce, both atypical of traditional steakhouse menus. Of course, a wide variety of juicy steaks (exclusively Prime aged) and chops are grilled to perfection and paired with such gorgeous complements as black tiger prawns, bacon-wrapped Diver scallops, roasted portobello mushrooms, and roasted peaches. Rounding out the experience are expert pours from

TOP LEFT Prime Porterhouse with tempura battered onion rings

TOP RIGHT Dessert sampler plate - Triple tier carrot cake, warm fudge chocolate cake, brown bag apple pie, Heath bar cheesecake, fresh berry martini.

BOTTOM LEFT Prime filet de Michael - 12oz filet with bacon-wrapped diver scallop and 2 Black Tiger prawns.

BOTTOM RIGHT Ceviche Tostada Royal - marinated seafood on won ton tostada with avocado.

the bar, fine wines in every price range, and classic desserts like crème brulée, berries with crème fraîche, fudge cake, and pecan pie.

With so much excellence in one place, it's no wonder that Perry's has earned accolades from *The Dallas Morning News, D Magazine, Wine Spectator, Gourmet,* the North American Restaurant Association, Distinguished Restaurants of North America, and was named to Tom Horan's Top Ten Club three consecutive years.

What to wear: People in Dallas like to get dressed up. We're not a blue jeans type of place; we're snazzier, snappy casual.

Q&A

MORE ABOUT AMIE AND TRAVIS ...

What personal indulgence do you spend the most money on?
Amie: Shoes.
Travis: Sunglasses.

What's one thing most people don't know about you?
Amie: I was a dance education major.
Travis: Not much — I am all out there.

Who has had the biggest influence on your career?
Amie: All the people who said I couldn't do it.
Travis: Mel Holland

Perry's Restaurant
2911 Routh Street
Dallas, TX 75201
214-871-9991
www.perrys-dallas.com

ROUGH CREEK LODGE

Gerard Thompson, executive chef and
director of food and beverage

At most restaurants, a regular customer is one who comes in once a week.
At Rough Creek Lodge, a regular customer is one who comes in three
times a day and for a week or more. "That's what sets us apart," says
executive chef Gerard Thompson, who just celebrated eight years with the
acclaimed destination resort. "It's much more exciting to cook for a guest
who's here for breakfast, lunch, and dinner, because they're getting three
different experiences."

It's also more of a challenge. To mix things up, Thompson changes the
lunch and dinner menus daily. "Our menu is very seasonal. We write the
menu with what's available," he says. The freshness of the food makes his
menus stand out: If striped marlin is what comes through the door, then it's
in; if peaches are in season, then he might serve peach dumplings for
dessert.

"We only have one small freezer, and that's for our homemade ice cream, so
we enjoy making everything from scratch, every day," says Thompson,
who's in the kitchen each morning, along with his team, who bakes artisan
breads (there are seven kinds), scones, croissants, doughnuts, and wedding
cakes.

He makes his own sausages, stocks, and soups. A local supplier brings
fresh eggs and even truffles from France during season. "We even smoke
our own fish here," he says. "I don't think people are expecting to see such
beautiful farm fresh produce, sushi-grade fish, and unbelievable breads
when they come out to the country," Thompson says. "We ship in our fish
fresh from Hawaii, fiddlehead ferns from Maine, morel mushrooms from
Michigan, and we have our own grower of micro greens and tomatoes here
locally."

Though the menu may constantly change, the food quality and service is
always impeccable. Whether serving a cup of tea, pouring soup tableside,
taking care of 300 guests at a sit-down wedding reception, or laying out a

ABOVE Dinner at sunset on the terrace
overlooking Mallard Lake and the 11,000+
acres here at Rough Creek Lodge and Resort
enjoy hiking, biking, four wheeling, horseback
riding, hunting or just star gazing by one of
our massive fire pits.

TOP LEFT Baked to order Hot Apple Cobbler with Ginger-Vanilla Bean ice cream and Apple Cider Sauce.

TOP RIGHT Grilled Texas Quail with Smoked Cheddar Cheese-Roasted Poblano Pepper Grits with Sherry Maple Glaze.

BOTTOM LEFT Game Bird Pot Au Fou with House made Pheasant Sausage.

BOTTOM RIGHT Butternut Squash Granny Smith Apple Soup with Smithfield Ham Biscuits.

RIGHT A comfortable chair in the "Great Room" to enjoy a Single malt Scotch after Bird or Deer hunting or a mint Julep after a horseback ride.

deli buffet for a corporate lunch for 12, the highest of standards is maintained. "Every meal is prepared by the same kitchen brigade and every party gets the same grand service," Thompson says. "We don't have a banquet staff or banquet servers; it's all blended into one. That's what separates Rough Creek Lodge from other hotels."

Thompson came to the Lone Star State after working seven years in Santa Barbara. He admits that he was a little jaded by Californians' attitudes toward food and calls Texans' approach to dining "quite refreshing." "I remember when we first opened and I was creating the menu for a group of 25 women. They wanted beef for lunch," he says, his voice still registering astonishment. "I'd never serve beef for lunch in Santa Barbara."

Texans, Thompson says, are adventurous eaters, and that makes his job more fun. "I love cooking in Texas. I can put sweetbreads on the menu. Tonight I have venison, duck, quail, and pheasant. And people will eat it." Texans also love dessert, he says, pointing out that 65 of 70 Rough Creek Lodge diners will end their meals with something sweet. "And we make some wonderful desserts."

Wonder, surprise, and delight seem to be a theme with Thompson; the same can be said for Rough Creek Lodge. Rated Most Outstanding Lodge in North America for 2005 by Condé Nast's Johansens and named to Condé Nast Traveller's list of Best Hotels in the World and the magazine's Gold List of the World's Best Places to Stay, the hotel itself is an unexpected 11,000 acre oasis 70 miles outside of Dallas. With soaring, 40-foot ceilings; floor-to-ceiling windows overlooking a miraculous lake; a massive 40-foot fireplace; Christofle silver; and Villeroy & Boch glassware, the restaurant is at once rustic and sophisticated, a combination that sets the dress code.

What to wear: "You don't need a jacket here; shorts and a shirt are perfectly fine," Thompson says.

MORE ABOUT GERARD ...

What is your favorite food?
Sushi, or just fish in general. I eat it probably twice a day.

What color best describes you?
Yellow. I think I am always in a great mood and easy to get along with.

If you weren't a chef, what would you be doing?
I would be an architect.

What personal indulgence do you spend the most money on?
Eating out and traveling.

Rough Creek Lodge
5165 County Road 2013
Glen Rose, TX 76043
800-864-4705
www.roughcreek.com

ABOVE The Sante Fe Room accommodates a private party of up to 40 people.

RIGHT Warm and inviting, Via Real draws a crowd six nights a week.

VIA REÁL

Fran Lively Mathers, owner and proprietor

In the year before Fran Lively Mathers became the owner of Via Reál, she was a regular customer. She loved dining there, and when she learned one Friday night that it was to be the restaurant's last, she set out to purchase the 15-month-old establishment. That was 20 years ago; and that's where the success story begins.

Since that time, Via Reál has evolved from its original 4,000-square-foot beginnings to a space more than twice that size in the heart of Las Colinas, on the south side of the Four Seasons Resort and Club. In addition to being the local watering hole, the restaurant serves an international clientele. And in the hugely competitive Dallas dining scene, it's remained on top for two decades, earning Zagat's highest billing three years in a row and being called "Las Colinas's most venerable Mexican restaurant" by *Texas Monthly.*

"Our mission is to give people a break from their reality. And I love making that happen: I love what I do. That's the key," Mathers says. Obviously, customers love what she does, too.

With seating for 250 guests, Via Reál serves lunch and dinner six days a week (on Saturdays only dinner is served) with a notable champagne brunch on Sundays. With four private dining rooms and a reputation for catering to movers and shakers, the restaurant hosts hundreds of corporate dinners and private celebrations each year.

The menu, flush with Southwestern and Tex-Mex classics with gourmet flair, features items like pecan-crusted Chilean sea bass, with jalapeno-pineapple sauce, served with chipotle potatoes, asparagus and baby carrots beautifully arranged in a carved quarter pineapple. The quaint bar serves a

TOP LEFT Via Réal sits just South of the Four Seasons in the Las Colinas Plaza.

TOP RIGHT Executive Chef Felipe Gaytan turns out delicious dishes; veteran waiter Diego Soto serves it up.

BOTTOM LEFT Owner Fran Lively Mathers is a restaunteur extraordinaire.

BOTTOM RIGHT Via Real's wine room- the Sedona - is perfect for intimate gathering of 10 to 20 people.

mean margarita made with the finest El Tesoro tequila, in signature "grande" hand-blown margarita glasses (imported from Mexico).

And the service is second to none. Diego Soto, serving guests since the restaurant's inception 20 years ago, is representative of the whole Via Reál experience. "People will wait an hour just to sit in his section," Mathers says. "He's loads of fun, booked every night, and takes care of everybody from the postman to Troy Aikman." In short, Soto, like Via Reál, is really something extraordinary.

What to wear: The food is upscale but the attire is Sante Fe style. I term it country club casual. We see everything from business suits to jeans and golf shirts. Just be comfortable.

MORE FROM FRAN ...

What is something most people don't know about you?
I am a country girl at heart. I love my ranch in the Texas Hill Country.

What color best describes you?
Yellow gold. I hope it reflects my sunny personality.

Via Reál
4020 North MacArthur Boulevard
Irving, TX 75038
972-650-9001
www.viareal.com

YORK

ABOVE Contemporary yet quaint, the dining room allows food and good company to be the focus.

RIGHT York Street's modern and colorful art pieces delightfully line its walls.

York Street

Sharon Hage, chef and owner

It's a hot July day, and the first plump heirloom tomatoes of the summer have just arrived at York Street's back door. "You won't find these on our menu in November," says Chef Sharon Hage, who's known for a strict approach to seasonal cooking. "We only have wild salmon on the menu when the salmon run in the spring," she adds. "Every August I serve wild blueberry pie. There's rhubarb in the spring, and right now we've got Noon Day sweet onions. In the fall we'll have pears for salads and desserts, and blood oranges in the winter. December 1 is the opening of the Maine Diver scallop season, and we always do something with them." She composes a new menu each day, which confounds some regulars who want their favorites to be available year-round. A purist? You bet. Hage wouldn't allow anything less. "It doesn't waiver with us. The seasons dictate what's on the menu," she says.

York Street is an intimate restaurant with only 12 tables and a pared down simple decor. "It's all about the company and the meal," says Hage. In a small space, some things fall by the wayside. Espresso, for instance. In its place, Hage serves specialty teas, which she carefully pairs with dishes, just like she does the wines she serves. How does this go over with the after-dinner-espresso crowd? "Our customers are game to try anything. If you come all the way over here to eat our sweetbreads, you'll try tea," she says.

York Street's customers are unique. Remember the wild blueberry pie that Hage bakes every August? "I've got someone on the books for August 20 who called three months in advance to make sure we'd have the pie when he came in."

What to wear: We just tell people to be comfortable. Come as you are.

York Street
6047 Lewis Street
Dallas, TX 75206
214-826-0968

Cibal, page177

CHAPTER FOUR
SAN ANTONIO

ABOVE Downstairs party room Abajo (Spanish for beneath) used predominately for private functions. Seats 50, opens up onto patio overlooking river walk.

RIGHT Private dining room Arriba (Spanish for above), seats up to 60, adjacent to mezzanine bar/lounge, overlooks main dining room, predominately for private functions, barreled walls covered in saltillo.

ÁCENAR MODERN TEXMEX

Lisa Wong, founder and CEO
James Sanchez, executive chef

A fresher, cooler, cutting-edge approach to what's been done thousands of times in Texas is what Lisa Wong set out to accomplish when she embarked on Ácenar. Not just another Mexican food restaurant, Ácenar is a highly stylized concept that showcases modern Tex-Mex in an environment that's sophisticated yet has all the energy and pizzazz of a south-of-the-border holiday.

Situated on what is, at least for now, a quiet stretch of the San Antonio Riverwalk, nestled next to Hotel Valencia, Ácenar is Wong's most aggressive effort to date. Opened in March 2004, with possibly the largest dining area on the Riverwalk (nearly half of that outside) and a bustling bar,

the restaurant was created in a "new generation" location, meaning no business had occupied the space before, so Wong and her partner, Peter Selig, could dream and create a concept that truly ignites your senses. "I always loved the Riverwalk. Never did I think I would own a piece of it," Wong says. And in a manner befitting the food it would serve, everything from the stained-concrete floor to the 22-foot-high ceiling was created from scratch. "It's exactly what we wanted."

At 41, Wong counts Ácenar as her fifth restaurant venture—she opened her first, Lisa's, at just 18. Focused and driven, she comes by her restaurant expertise naturally: The business runs in her family. Before she was born,

LEFT Lenticular wall. Words for food ingredients commonly found in Latin kitchens. Located in main dining room, can be viewed from mezzanine as well.

FACING PAGE LEFT Features the mocajete wall - a mocajete is the stone bowl used to grind items making food (i.e. guacamole) it is the outside entrance into the restaurant, overlooking the river walk.

FACING PAGE RIGHT Wall in main dining room, relfecting the style of a Girard textile, a combination of woods, including oak and walnut.

her grandfather, Gow Wong, was the proud owner of Sung Lee Café just down the street from Acnear, on Commerce. And her abuelita, "Mama" Luisa, prepared a Mexican feast for the family every Sunday afternoon. Thusly, she inherited her grandfather's entrepreneurial spirit and her grandmother's flair with food.

"The kitchen is the heart and soul of any successful restaurant," Wong says. Overseeing heart and soul at Ácenar is San Antonio-born and -raised James Sanchez. An honors graduate from the Culinary Institute of America, the up-and-comer worked at the Hyatt Hill Country Resort and as executive chef at Central Market before becoming Ácenar's chef. Sanchez's food is "an amazing array of tastes derived from the cross-cultural influence that is reflective of our city," Wong says. House specialties include duck chorizo chalupas, steam-roasted cabrito, and entomatadas—tacos filled with chicken and sweet potato—as well as an exquisite cinnamon-spiked chocolate mousse. A Sunday mariachi brunch features a chilaquile station, where guests create their own egg dishes with grilled meats, cheeses, peppers, veggies, and tortilla strips.

The kicky cuisine is matched perfectly by the restaurant's interior, which Wong calls "eye spice." Designed by architect Henry Muñoz and inspired by the clever midcentury textiles of Alexander Girard and his work for New York's La Fonda del Sol, the décor at Ácenar is playful and full of movement. Natural wood offsets vibrant reds, hot pinks, acid greens, and bright oranges. Nearly every surface is curved, and a 25 foot long lenticular wall dominates the main dining room, subtly alternating between Spanish and English words.

Of course, too many drinks from Átomar and those mingling words might be a little more difficult to decipher. The Houston Street-level bar draws a hip, happening crowd for watermelon mojitos, blood orange martinis, and tuna margaritas (made with cactus flower, not fish!).

What to wear: Something fun. Something sassy. Casual but classy.

MORE ABOUT LISA ...

What is one thing most people don't know about you?

I am shy.

Do you think your name fits you?

No. I look Latin, but my maiden name is Chinese, and I own a Mexican restaurant.

What do you do to bring a meal cooked at home to life?

Put on some good music, light a few candles, and serve your food on fine china.

Ácenar Modern TexMex
146 East Houston Street
San Antonio, TX 78205
210-222-2362
www.acenar.com

ABOVE Indigenous touches, like locally grown gourds, give diners a Texas perspective on the otherwise "big city" decor.

ABOVE RIGHT The cresent shaped mezzanine, adorned with prayer candles, is a favorite for couples looking for a romantic evening.

BELOW RIGHT The floor to ceiling windows give guests inside an equally impressive view of the Riverwalk below.

FAR RIGHT Contemporary decor compliments the loft-like space of Biga.

BIGA ON THE BANKS

Bruce Auden, executive chef and proprietor

When Bruce Auden moved from Chicago to Texas in 1983, his pioneering reputation followed him. Today, that reputation precedes him. There are few on the fine dining scene who haven't heard of the London-born restaurateur's extraordinary cuisine.

Called "the patriarch of San Antonio chefs" by a counterpart, Auden continues to create dishes both adventuresome and divine at Biga on the Banks. The five-time James Beard nominee is as modest as he is charming, but there's nothing humble about the exquisite experience found at his destination restaurant.

Albeit on the Riverwalk, Biga operates on a quiet stretch, high above the water. It's not the sort of place one stumbles upon, but those lucky enough to know of it are rewarded with a beautiful loft-like dining room, contemporary but far from severe, and a view as stunning as the food. Favorites include Axis venison with Brussels sprouts and goat cheese strudel, the you-have-to-ask-because-it's-not-on-the-menu Expensive Mushrooms, and toffee pudding, which had a *New York Times* reporter begging for more.

What to wear: "Whatever you are comfortable in. A tux is fine; shorts and a T-shirt is fine, too," says Auden.

Biga on the Banks
203 South Saint Mary's Street
San Antonio, TX 78205
210-225-0722
www.biga.com

ABOVE Boudro's kitchen turns out flavorful, hearty dishes like mesquite-grilled Texas quail with wild mushroom stuffing.

RIGHT Avocados, lemons, limes and other fresh ingredients make guacamole prepared tableside a favorite among guests.

Once called "a best-kept secret" by the press, Boudro's is now a much-talked-about hot spot, brimming with beautiful people day and night, including the occasional celebrity.

The busy little bistro serves cutting-edge Contemporary Regional cuisine. Its chef artfully fuses the influences of Mexico, East Texas, Louisiana, and the Germanic Texas Hill Country; and the kitchen uses locally sourced produce, meat, and seafood to turn out such divine dishes as smoked shrimp enchiladas, blackened prime rib with Boudreaux butter, rosemary-grilled yellowfin tuna with lime-cilantro butter, and pan-fried Texas crab cakes. Labeled "starters," cocktails range from hurricanes and bloody Marys to prickly pear margaritas and Texas tea. But many guests start with

fresh guacamole, made tableside by servers who never seem to tire of whipping up the perennial pleaser.

Guests can dine inside, among granite walls and primitive iron artwork; riverside, under out-of-the-ordinary umbrellas; or, if they call ahead, on the water, on one of Boudro's own river barges. More than just a destination for tourists and conventioneers, even San Antonio locals list the surprising Riverwalk restaurant among their favorites.

What to wear: Something comfortable, casual, and fashionable—just like the restaurant itself.

Boudro's
421 East Commerce
San Antonio, TX 78205
210-224-8484
www.boudros.com

ABOVE Vibrant blown glass by a local artist, a custom chandelier by Gini Garcia, and colorful oil paintings create an opulent environment at Cibal.

RIGHT A wide selection of fine wines complements specialty dishes like Vuelve a la vida (a ceriche medley) and a grilled tuna with vegetables with mango sauce.

CIBAL

Jorge Cosio Seifer, operations manager

The name "Cibal" is derived from the Greek word for the residents of the ancient city of Sybaris, who were self-indulgent, hedonistic people devoted to pleasure and luxury. Such a name, then, gives guests a certain expectation for Cibal. Both the interior design and the menu are eclectic feasts.

Though the restaurant name is Greek, the kitchen specializes in steaks and pasta, with influences from the world over. Choose from an outside skirt steak with guacamole or sirloin medallions with a buttery raspberry sauce. Design-your-own pasta dishes let diners mix and match noodles and sauces. And then there are the empanadas, Peking duck tacos, and desserts like tres leches cake and a chocolate bombe with a molten truffle center.

Eat inside—where a colorful, handblown glass chandelier hangs in proximity to ceiling panels comprising wine bottles n steel frames, and modern, laser-cut screens contrast with original paintings, equally bold but more traditional. Or dine outside on the patio, a shady respite with wicker furniture and a gurgling water sculpture bearing the restaurant's name.

What to wear: There's no need to dress fancy, casual c othes are fine.

Cibal
4003 Broadway
San Antonio, TX 78209
210-822-8311

ABOVE Citrus serves gulf shrimp, prime tenderloin and more in a smart, sophisticated setting.

RIGHT Hotel Valencia's restaurant, Citrus, specializes in New American cuisine, offering fine dining as well as lighter fare.

CITRUS

Jeffrey Balfour, executive chef

A gem within a gem, Citrus resides inside the Hotel Valencia Riverwalk, a boutique hotel on the San Antonio Riverwalk. And if Citrus is a diamond, Jeff Balfour is the culet—the point of origin or, in this case, the chef of origin for brilliance.

Thirty-two, vivacious, and handsome, Balfour describes himself as low-key, but he gets his kicks while cooking. "The whole thing to me means having fun," he says of the restaurant business. "I am very lucky to do what I love." That passion was first realized 11 years ago under Tim Keating's tutelage at LaReserve in Houston. "I basically bugged him until he let me into his kitchen. I learned all of the basics from him."

At Citrus, Balfour prepares savory, imaginative New American dishes like oven-baked sea bass with wild roasted mushrooms, croissant bread pudding, and foie gras butter sauce; South Texas ostrich with meat gravy, broccoli rabe, and smoked heirloom tomatoes; and pan-seared diver scallops on a bed of jumbo shrimp risotto with a tomato and basil shellfish reduction. "If you see something you like, you'd better try it," Balfour says. No dish stays on the menu more than a few months.

What to wear: "Most of our guests are out on the town, dressed casually but upscale," Balfour says.

Citrus
Hotel Valencia Riverwalk
150 East Houston Street
San Antonio, TX 78205
210-230-8412
www.hotelvalencia.com

ABOVE L'Etoile's open, eclectic architecture, progressive cuisine, and impressive wine list create the perfect setting for both business and romantic dinners.

RIGHT Thierry Burkle and his family of polite staff memebers.

L'ETOILE

Thierry Burkle, executive chef and co-owner

Thierry Burkle, executive chef and co-owner of L'Etoile, believes that "like fine art, food is a distinctive extension of personality. Each gourmet presentation is as unique and exciting as the clientele, family, and friends who constantly inspire our culinary creations."

For 20 years, L'Etoile has provided San Antonians with affordable, award-winning cuisine. Its reputation is founded upon an unstinting devotion to clientele and a passion for fine food. This proud heritage has inspired Burkle to create dishes ranging from classic to eclectic, with a culinary flair for blending simplicity and sophistication.

What to wear: L'Etoile's atmosphere is one of casual elegance. No coat or tie required.

L'Etoile
6106 Broadway
San Antonio, TX 78209
210-826-4551
www.letoilesa.com

ABOVE As one might expect, Restaurant Le Reve has a dreamy quality befitting its name.

RIGHT Chef Andrew Weissman and a talented staff make every meal an event.

RIGHT Food is presented on Andrew's collection of unique plates from around the world.

RIGHT Elegant stemware, ready for chef's tasting menu.

RESTAURANT LE RÊVE

Andrew Weissman, proprietor and executive chef

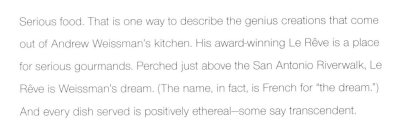

Serious food. That is one way to describe the genius creations that come out of Andrew Weissman's kitchen. His award-winning Le Rêve is a place for serious gourmands. Perched just above the San Antonio Riverwalk, Le Rêve is Weissman's dream. (The name, in fact, is French for "the dream.") And every dish served is positively ethereal—some say transcendent.

A rising star in the culinary world, the 37-year-old journalist-turned-chef starts with pristine ingredients and builds on classic techniques to create unparalleled contemporary French cuisine. The menu is dictated by the season and market availability. Georges Bank monkfish tail on melted Napa cabbage with maple-glazed pancetta and tournedo of Angus beef with foie gras custard and sauce Medoc are just a couple of the plats de résistance on one night's menu.

Those lucky enough to score one of the handful of tables can expect a relaxed, candlelit evening, with dinner lasting two to three hours. Orders are prepared a la minute, nothing is ever sliced, seasoned, or sautéed ahead of time. Everything is done under Weissman's watchful eye. He has worked the line every single night for the seven years that Le Rêve has been open.

What to wear: Not only is it the only Mobil four-star restaurant in San Antonio, it's also the only restaurant in the city that requires men to wear jackets.

Restaurant Le Rêve
152 East Pecan Street
San Antonio, TX 78205
210-212-2221
www.restaurantlereve.com

ABOVE Cast iron seared Alaskan halibut with fava beans, purple Peruvian potatoes, oven roasted tomatoes and sweet basil oil.

RIGHT The glowing unparalleled ambiance of The Lodge Restaurant of Castle Hills.

THE LODGE RESTAURANT OF CASTLE HILLS

Jason Dady, executive chef and owner
Jake Dady, partner
Tommy Zachry, partner

For Chef Jason Dady, life and work are all about balance. On the menu, there's as much fresh seafood as wild game and red meat. He's as experimental with exotic dishes as he is committed to serving customers' favorites. Look for spicy Asian dishes along with good ol' Texas center cut, cast iron cooked beef filet. New World wines from California and Washington state share the wine menu with Old World classics from Italy, France and Germany. Hot appetizers. Cold appetizers. Yin with the Yang.

When it comes to people, Dady always strikes a perfect balance. "Our location is unparalleled, our food is great, but our service and our staff are what really separates us from our competition," says Dady. "Take care of

your employees and they will take care of your customers and you." Dady closes the Lodge for every major holiday to give his employees time off with their families, and Sundays are reserved for family and friends.

At 28, Dady is young, but he's got plenty of experience to go with his wisdom. After earning a degree in restaurant and hotel management from Texas Tech University, he studied at the prestigious California Culinary Academy in San Francisco, and later worked at the renowned Stars Bar and Dining and at Beringer Wine Estate in Napa Valley. "I was raised in the hospitality industry (his grandparents were in the business) so when I decided to make that my career, it was 100 miles per hour all the way."

Dady was 24 when he opened The Lodge in San Antonio in 2001. To his great joy, the restaurant has become a family oriented business, with his brother, wife, in-laws and mother all involved.

The restaurant is housed inside an historic 1929 stone mansion, set on 2 1/2 acres and shaded by almost 200 oak trees. "People drive by two or three times before they realize it's there," says Dady. "It looks like a really nice house, not a restaurant." I wanted to make the restaurant as comfortable as walking into someone's home," says Dady. Rooms in the twostory house were turned into intimate dining areas, each seating 8 to 16 people. A stone guest house in the back serves as a private dinner cottage that hosts up to 25, while several hundred people can be entertained on the grounds of the estate for weddings or other large events.

The Lodge has two seatings each evening, and a course-style menu of three or five courses. A chef tasting menu consists of seven signature dishes, including grilled Bobwhite quail with Maytag blue cheese, grilled apple, basil oil, and Fredericksburg peach salsa in summer (in the fall, it's fresh Bartlett pears). Another signature dish is Maple Leaf Farms duck confit with orecchiette pasta, sweet corn, Italian parsley and toasted garlic bread crumbs.

TOP LEFT Pan-seared duck breast with spring asparagus, sweet potato and celery root ragout with ancho chili vinaigrette.

TOP RIGHT Hand built in 1929. The Lodge Restaurant is surrounded by a wrought iron and Cibolo Creek rock gate. The Lodge Restaurant sandblasted a small sign to fit right in with the natural beauty of the property.

BOTTOM LEFT The Lodge Restaurant is designed to make you feel right at home. The furniture and fixtures all fit right into the ambiance that the property provides.

BOTTOM RIGHT Executive Chef/Owner Jason Dady.

FACING PAGE Private and cozy dining rooms make The Lodge a perfect venue for small private parties or intimate affairs.

ABOVE The Lodge Restaurant showcases a local artist, Alejandra Martinez and her amazing oil paintings.

FACING PAGE The staircase leading upstairs to the private dining rooms is lit to showcase the amazing architecture of the home. The original radiators and velvet rope lining the staircase add to the showstopping and heartwarming feel.

"I would describe our menu as New American with French and Italian influences," says Dady, who remembers how the folks in San Antonio were at first perplexed by his take on food. "San Antonio at the time was a little further behind on the culinary frontier, but it allowed us to come and make a name for ourselves without a lot of competition," says Dady. "As crazy as it sounds, even duck breast was a hard sell when we first opened." Now four years later, the community which was reluctant to try his seared foie gras with red wine braised oxtail, embraces it fondly.

What to wear: "San Antonio business casual," says Dady. "We have a lot of people celebrating anniversaries and important events, so I always tell people to dress comfortably but dress up nice."

MORE ABOUT JASON ...

What personal indulgence do you spend the most money on?
Golf, fishing, and poker games.

Name one thing most people don't know about you.
I love being a dad more than a chef.

Do you think your name fits you, and why?
Pronounced "Day-Dee" but spelled Dady...leads right into "Who's Your Dady." Works great!

What color best describes you and why?
Yellow, always happy and energetic.

What is the highest compliment you've received professionally?
"This is the best meal of my life." You cannot top that. Period.

What is the most unusual culinary technique you've applied to your creations?
Toasted garlic cotton candy for a porcini-crusted lamb loin.

The Lodge Restaurant of Castle Hills
1746 Lockhill Selma Road
San Antonio, TX 78213
210-349-8466

ABOVE Main dining area – dessert is "Chocolate Soufflé".

RIGHT Top dish – Field Green Salad with red onion, English cucumber, cherry tomatoes, croutons & Dijon walnut dressing. Bottom dish – Filet of Grilled Black Angus Beef Tenderloin with blue cheese mashed potatoes, grilled asparagus, crispy shallot rings & Mushroom-Cabernet sauce.

SILO ELEVATED CUISINE

Patrick Richardson, proprietor
Gus Ortiz, executive chef

At San Antonio's acclaimed Silo Elevated Cuisine, the ambiance is stylish and the food is superb. And that's as it should be: Both reflect proprietor Patrick Richardson's well-traveled background. In the restaurant business since 1983, Richardson has taken the best of what he earned in California, New York, and Chicago and created a dining experience worthy of its affluent Alamo Heights neighborhood.

From its unusual architecture to its seasoned staff, from trendy fusion cuisine to an all-encompassing approach to a night out, Silo is a rarity. The brick building that houses the restaurant resembles a grain silo, though it never functioned as one. Instead, it once was home to a bustling farmer's market, which has since been replaced with a lively bar. Though the contemporary, white-tablecloth restaurant

originally began as an avenue for the fresh fruits and vegetables, meats, cheeses, and other products sold at the market, the dining room now overlooks the spacious nightspot. An elevator transports guests to a glassed-in balcony that provides an elegant respite with a view of the lounge below.

In the kitchen, executive chef Gus Ortiz works magic with local and "imported" products. Prior to taking the helm at Silo, Ortiz worked under the tutelage of five-time James Beard-nominee Bruce Auden for 15 years. At Silo, Ortiz turns out food that impresses professional and amateur gourmands alike. Critics have raved about the salad of Bose pears stuffed with warm seafood and accessorized with raspberries, Cambozola cheese, and sherry vinaigrette. The chipotle marinated pork tenderloin on white cheddar grits with queso fresco, Texas peach chutney and an ancho chili-dried cherry sauce also is a standout. And pecan-crusted duck breast with Hudson Valley foie gras over a sweet corn-peach custard and huckleberry brandy sauce makes mouths water.

Just as the menu changes with available ingredients and the imagination of the chef, the dining room also gets continually updated with a showcase of regional artists' work, exhibits of which rotate quarterly. "When guests frequent a place often—and many of ours do, because we are such an integral part of the community—this ever-changing museum approach means

LEFT Silo bar area.

RIGHT Spicy Black Angus Beef Tenderloin Lettuce Wraps with Chili and Mint.

TOP LEFT Aromatic Braised Chilean Sea Bass on Crab Saffron Risotto Cake and Mussel-Lemongrass-Tomato Bouillon.

TOP RIGHT Wasabi Tempura Black Tiger Prawn with an English Cucumber-Seaweed Salad, Wasabi Mayo and Green Tobiko. Lower dish – Surf & Turf Oak grilled Black Angus Beef Tenderloin with Maine Lobster Tail over Three Potato-Wild Mushroom Gratin, Asparagus and Red Wine Reduction.

BOTTOM LEFT Cream Brulé Napoleon – background painting – Artist Teri Wright.

BOTTOM RIGHT Chocolate Soufflé.

constant appeal," Richardson says. And it's just one example of how Silo maintains its celebrated status. Another is the restaurant's lively bar scene.

After a meal of chicken-fried oysters on angel hair pasta with applewood-smoked bacon and tart apples or grilled Black Angus tenderloin with blue cheese mashed potatoes and asparagus, guests often linger for an after-dinner cognac or a specialty drink, like the Gorgeous Martini, and dance the night away in the bottom-floor bar. And that's the idea: "You come for a cocktail before, a fabulous meal, and stay for the live music in the bar after. Everything you need for a beautiful evening is right here," Richardson says.

What to wear: Upscale dining is played back in diners' attire. Be comfortable but look nice. Jeans are fine, but if you want to wear elegant attire, you won't feel out of place.

ABOVE Aromatic Braised Chilean Sea Bass on Crab Saffron Risotto Cake and Mussel-Lemongrass-Tomato Bouillon in the Blue Room, which accommodates approximately 100. Paintings by artist Teri Wright.

MORE ABOUT SILO ...

What is one of the more unusual things ever served at Silo?

"People were really surprised by the scallop ravioli," says executive chef Gus Ortiz. "It was an idea that I came up with while experimenting at home: scallops sliced paper-thin, stuffed with lobster meat and wild mushrooms. There is no pasta in sight. I serve it with a truffled porcini mushroom jus."

What separates Silo from the competition?

"We have the most unique dining experience in San Antonio. We are considered the local, chef-driven restaurant of choice," says proprietor Patrick Richardson.

"The complete package—quality of product, service, and atmosphere that includes art openings and live music—is what makes us remarkable."

What won't you find at the all-encompassing Silo?

Ortiz in the kitchen on Sundays. An accomplished soccer player, the 31-year-old father of two has been the San Antonio Soccer League's leading scorer for three consecutive years, scoring 47 goals one season. He takes Sundays off, leaving the cooking to his skilled, seasoned staff, and takes to the field.

Silo Elevated Cuisine
1133 Austin Highway
San Antonio, TX 78209
210-824-8686
www.siloelevatedcuisine.com

Uptown Sushi, page 219

CHAPTER FIVE
HOUSTON

ABOVE Roasted Chicken with watercress and barley salad.

RIGHT View of fountain on patio with solarium lit up in the background.

BACKSTREET CAFÉ

Tracy Vaught, proprietor
Hugo Ortega, executive chef

Although opened as a simple neighborhood watering hole more than 20 years ago, Backstreet Café has evolved into one of Houston's best-loved restaurants, known for an award-winning New American menu, celebrated wine list, romantic fireplaces, and patios that host the city's best alfresco dining.

Nestled on the edge of prestigious River Oaks in a 1930s house, the building's backstreet hideaway was ideal for geologist-turned-restaurateur Tracy Vaught. The charming eatery features a handsome bar, sunny solarium, and several intimate dining areas. A pleasant staff makes guests feel at home.

Lunch favorites include the lobster sandwich, crabmeat salad, and red corn enchiladas. At dinner, pan-seared duck breast, tenderloin with wild mushroom tamal, and garlic shrimp over jalapeno-cheese grits take center stage along with the nightly specials. The New Orleans-style courtyards become a lively Sunday retreat with a jazz brunch featuring specialty cocktails and a special menu.

What to wear: It's business casual during the day, a little more dressy at night.

Backstreet Café
1103 South Shepherd Drive
Houston, TX 77019
713-521-2239
www.backstreetcafe.net

ABOVE Dark woods populate the sophisticated interior designed by Candice Schiller.

NEAR RIGHT Chef Robert Del Grande.

FAR RIGHT Wood Grilled Shrimp is a spectacular treat at Café Annie.

CAFÉ ANNIE

Robert Del Grande, executive chef and proprietor

Serendipity led Robert Del Grande to be a chef. He didn't plan to own and operate one of the finest dining establishments in the nation or help found a pioneering enterprise that would alter the culinary landscape. But after grad school, he followed Mimi Kinsman, who would later become his wife and business partner, to Houston, where he was bitten by the restaurant bug and abandoned his biochemist aspirations. Twenty-five years later, the California native consistently wows guests with fresh takes on Southwestern flavors and efficient service in a charming and convivial atmosphere.

An easygoing idea guy, his last name fits him well. Realizing new concepts is Del Grande's favorite part of being in the kitchen. "You can have an idea in the morning and be serving it that evening. Just begin with an unfettered imagination, then use reason and determination to make it a reality." And the reality is that the award-winning Houston icon has been a dream for the accidental chef—and the patrons who dine here.

What to wear: Cafe Annie accommodates diners in dress ranging from blue jeans to ball gowns. City chic is the attire of choice at Bar Annie, while the main dining room tends to draw a more formally dressed crowd.

Cafe Annie
1728 Post Oak Boulevard
Houston, TX 77056
713-840-1111
www.cafe-annie.com

ABOVE A beautifully customized interior greets guests as they embark on a culinary adventure.

FACING PAGE LEFT Signature appetizer, Stuffed Avocado Prawn

FACING PAGE RIGHT An imported chariot fills overhead space and ancient faux stone murals adorn the walls.

CAFÉ LE JADEITE

Randy Chou, proprietor

Mixing what's traditionally Asian with elements of the contemporary West, Café Le Jadeite is a feast for both sight and taste. The dramatic decor, which impresses even before guests enter the restaurant and catches the eyes of passersby in Houston's River Oaks, creates an expectation for what's happening in the kitchen. Stone horses, glass room dividers etched with Chinese characters, green glass sculptures, crystal Buddha heads, and a two-story cascade of translucent red globes come together in a fantastical Shangri-La.

And what the interior designers have promised, the chefs—one from China, the other from Italy—deliver. With a menu that's decidedly Chinese, but not entirely so, proprietor Randy Chou's two-year-old restaurant serves the finest fusion this side of Shanghai. "We take a broader approach to Asian cuisine," Chou says, "along with specialties from France and Italy." As dazzling on the plate as they are delicious on the palate, Chou's favorites include a stuffed avocado prawn appetizer, pureed pumpkin seafood soup Chilean sea bass, and Hunan-style prawns and scallops.

What to wear: "Workaday wear is standard attire for guests," Chou says.

Café Le Jadeite
1952 West Gray
Houston, TX 77019
713-528-4288
www.cafelejadeite.biz

ABOVE As the restaurant's unique design feature, Carmelo has incorporated a miniature town based on his native Sicilian village of Taormina, where the exhausted, enchanted and enlightened traveler finds rest, refuge and pampering.

RIGHT Pino Virga, the Pied Piper of Taorimina, and Carmelo welcome Santa Claus and many other partygoers every holiday season for memorable dinners and celebrations.

CARMELO'S RISTORANTE

Carmelo Mauro, proprietor

"The secret of our authentic Italian cuisine is the marriage of proudly individual flavors," says Carmelo Mauro, who with his wife, Hilary, opened his romantic, Old-World restaurant in Houston in 1981, after spending 20 years in hotels and restaurants all over the globe.

The menu comprises appetizers such as fried calamari and artichoke bottoms filled with crab meat and almonds; homemade pastas such as Caribbean lobster-filled ravioli, fettucine with spicy veal ragu, and cannelloni filled with spinach and topped with cream and marinara sauce; seafood dishes such as red snapper with vermouth-mango sauce and tuna over fresh fennel mashed potatoes; and grilled meats such as lamb chops and sirloin strip. Complementing the food is an extensive wine list that features

more than 100 Italian varietals, more than 50 selections from California, as well as Texas wines and champagne.

In addition to providing them with great food, Mauro believes in giving his guests the "V.I.P." (Very Italian Pampering) treatment: breath mints, latte mugs, reading glasses, flashlights, and silk/cashmere shawls are special touches that make dining at Carmelo's like being at a good friend's house.

What to wear: "Dress is casual and comfortable, just like our restaurant," Mauro says.

Carmelo's Ristorante
14795 Memorial Drive
Houston, TX 77079
281-531-0696
www.carmelosrestaurant.com

ABOVE The Bar at Hugo's.

RIGHT Tikin Xic - achiote rubbed grouper, grilled in a banana leaf and served with arroz negro, jicama salad and pickled onions.

HUGO'S

Hugo Ortega, executive chef
Tracy Vaught, proprietor

With the opening of Hugo's, chef Hugo Ortega journeyed full circle to rediscover the foods of his homeland. He left Mexico as a teen seeking the American Dream and worked his way from dishwasher to executive chef, graduating from culinary school along the way. There, he mastered traditional cooking but always carried Mexico in his heart.

Even with two kitchens to oversee (he is also executive chef at Backstreet Café), Ortega can be found in Hugo's kitchen each day. Described by colleagues as a charming man who "cooks with his heart and soul,"

Ortega brings the exciting flavors of Mexico across the border with his Regional Mexican cuisine. Dishes are diverse—as light and fresh as a seafood cocktail prepared by fishermen on the beach, as deep and complex as the moles of Oaxaca, and as earthy as the simplest homemade corn tortilla.

What to wear: The crowd is young and hip. Guys wear jeans; the ladies tend to wear something a little more chic.

Hugo's
1600 Westheimer Road
Houston, TX 77006
713-524-7744
www.hugosrestaurant.net

ABOVE Main dining room of Gothic style with 24 foot arched vault ceiling; also shown, The Loft, a semi-private dining room, overlooking it.

LEFT One of the many exquisite desserts found at Mark's.

RIGHT Savory corn soufflé topped with avruga caviar and micro golden corn shoots, Nantucket Cape and Diver Scallops with a Chardonnay herb sauce.

MARK'S AMERICAN CUISINE

Mark Cox, owner and executive chef

A West Virginia native turned Houstonian and ever the man his customers and employees can count on, owner/chef Mark Cox is the consummate Southerner. It shows in his restaurant's location (a former house of worship), the way he treats his guests (like friends), and especially in the menu at his award-winning namesake restaurant, Mark's American Cuisine.

"All chefs dream of owning their own restaurant," says Cox, who by age 25 was Executive Chef at Brennan's of Houston. Cox joined the Vallone Restaurant Group in 1985, working there for 11 years before venturing out on his own. With assistance from his wife, Lisa, he opened Mark's in a risky location, a renovated church in Montrose, in July 1997. But the good word

of Cox's inventive cuisine spread like wildfire and "in less than a month we had weekend reservations booked two to three weeks out," Cox remembers.

The food, which Cox calls American Seasonal, draws inspiration from many lands, but his Southern accent is prevalent in dishes such as the Kentucky bourbon-glazed pork tenderloin, the fire-roasted chicken breast over Mississippi-style grits, and seasonal desserts like strawberry shortcake, prepared to order with homemade biscuits.

What to wear: Coat and tie not required. Shorts and ball caps not permitted.

Mark's American Cuisine
1658 Westheimer Road
Houston, TX 77006
713-523-3800
www.marks1658.com

NINO'S RESTAURANT

Vincent and Mary Mandola, proprietors

From his second-floor office, Vincent Mandola watches the comers and goers, not much caring which of his family's Italian triumvirate customers choose–Nino's, or Grappino di Nino—just as long as they enjoy their meals, tell all their friends, and come back for more. And they've done all those things since 1977, when he and his wife, Mary, opened their first restaurant, Nino's.

At the time, there were few casual Italian restaurants in Houston. Recognizing a need, the second-generation Italian-American bought a two-story building on the west side of downtown and, borrowing from a few family recipes, started serving sandwiches, pizza, and pasta. Demand for tasty regional Italian dishes, like osso bucco (served with risotto), rosemary chicken (cooked over a wood-burning rotisserie), and innovations such as Veal Vincent (sautéed with artichoke hearts and lemon butter), grew fast. By its fifth year, the restaurant had begun seating on the second floor, but the space still overflowed.

So, in 1984, the Mandolas opened a second dining spot, Vincent s Restaurant. And when they needed a private dining space, they expanded again, in 1996, opening Grappino di Nino, a private banquet and wine room. The grappa bar and outdoor patio quickly became a popular happy hour spot. Nino's added dining and a wood-burning pizza oven to its own newly renovated bar in 2000, furthering its evolution as a favorite Houston dining spot.

What to wear: Dressy casual.

Nino's Restaurant
2817 West Dallas Street
Houston, TX 77019
713-522-5120
www.ninos-vincents.com

LEFT Split level "dining nooks" provide groups with great views of the wild game mounts and natural wood finishes.

RIGHT Dine al fresco with backdrop of waterfalls and a gazebo.

RAINBOW LODGE

Donnette Hansen, proprietor

In an era of fewer and fewer independently owned restaurants, Rainbow Lodge is at once dependable and refreshing. From the moment guests set foot on the stunning two-acre grounds, replete with lush landscaping, waterfalls, a small pond, and a romantic gazebo, until the time they drive away, inevitably with satisfied smiles on their faces, the commitment of owner Donnette Hansen shines through. The 18-year restaurant veteran has remained focused on the details of providing fine food and wine in an unforgettable setting, even as the city has grown up around the Houston landmark's woodsy location on the banks of Buffalo Bayou.

An avid fly-fisher for 20 years, Hansen's passion for the sport is evident everywhere in her restaurant: from the very name—rainbow, after the trout—

to the fresh and saltwater mounts on the dining room walls to the hand-carved, glass-top bar resembling a stream. Built by a Vermont artist, the bar is something Hansen is particularly proud of. "It's something people see and talk about afterward."

A drink in the Tied Fly Bar often precedes dinner, and people with a penchant for romance book the tiny table in the back of the wine cellar; it's reserved every night for marriage proposals and wedding anniversaries, Hansen says. "It's the sexiest spot in the house." But there are many private nooks perfect for lovers in the rustic split-level dining room. Rainbow Lodge is often lauded by national and local publications as the most romantic in town.

BOTTOM LEFT Grilled Shrimp on Tempura Risotto "Roll" with Saffron Cream.

BOTTOM RIGHT "Citrus Grove" a refreshing summer dessert. Meyer Lemon Tart, Key Lime Sorbet and Chilled Mandarin Orange Soup.

Its wine cellar also makes frequent appearances on "best" lists, including that of *Wine Spectator* magazine, which has awarded the restaurant its Award of Excellence for 12 years running. Completing the picture of perfection is a menu second to none. Seafood and wild game-centric, the food furthers the hunting-and-fishing theme. Favorite dishes include the mixed grill, with venison, duck, elk, and wild boar, and the pan-seared red snapper served with crab and cheddar grits. Top dinner off with The Nudge, a coffee drink with Kahlua, brandy, amaretto, and fresh whipped cream—perfect fireside on a chilly winter's night.

What to wear: A smile; and something comfortable and stylish, something you can relax in and enjoy your meal.

Q&A

MORE ABOUT
DONNETTE ...

What do you like most about doing business in Texas?
People are friendly and casual, and a handshake goes a long way.

What's the easiest way to give a meal cooked at home pizzazz?
Serve it outside and pair it with a great wine.

Rainbow Lodge
1 Birdsall
Houston, TX 77007
713-861-8666
www.rainbow-lodge.com

TOP The upper level of the main dining room overlooking Buffalo Bayou

BOTTOM Aged purple cedar handrails lead the way to the "Tied Fly Bar," Hansen's custom handcarved trout stream.

ABOVE Dining Room - Unparalleled cuisine, major wine list and pampering service set the stage for one of America's great restaurants.

ABOVE RIGHT Dining Room - a cascading waterwall with an open kitchen and world class art.

FAR RIGHT Wine Library - an intimate gorgeous room that seats up to 10 people surrounded by great wines and a Murano chandelier, perfect for private dinners or meetings.

TONY'S

Tony Vallone, proprietor
Olivier Ciesielski, chef

Tony Vallone has served six presidents, Kirk Douglas, Robert De Niro, Dustin Hoffman, John Travolta, Frank Sinatra, and every socialite in town. His namesake restaurant is where Houston's elite go to see and be seen, and it's where even the most ordinary residents celebrate birthdays and anniversaries. In short, Tony's is an impressive jewel worthy of America's royalty.

With a passion for perfection and a relentless pledge to pursue only the best—whether in food quality, presentation, service, or atmosphere—Vallone has for nearly 35 years been the indisputable king of his home city's dining scene. The award-winning wine list is vast: 850 selections strong. "There may be larger lists," Vallone says, "but none is more comprehensive or offers better buys." The continental menu has a heavy Italian influence, and it changes seasonally. Late summer saw Olivier Ciesielski turning out beef short ribs with mashed potatoes aioli, salt-

crusted snapper in a red wine reduction, and zucchini blossoms stuffed with lump crabmeat and sauteed with a mild buerre blanc. Of course, anyone who's a regular at Tony's can tell you that the signature osso buc is second to none, the 30 days naturally aged Prime steaks are divine, and the center-cut veal chop (a favorite of former President Bill Clinton) should not be missed.

Always up for a culinary challenge, Ciesielski will make anything a guest desires. "You name it, we make it," Vallone says. "Except maybe chicken fried steak—I just can't get it right."

What to wear: Vallone recommends a jacket for men (a tie is optional), and women always look beautiful—after all, it's Texas.

Tony's
3755 Richmond Avenue
Houston, TX 77046
713-622-6778
www.tonyshouston.com

ABOVE Frontal entrance view of Sea Anemone lights.

RIGHT Main dining area view from lower level.

UPTOWN SUSHI

Donald Chang, proprietor and executive chef

Donald Chang is a man who gives 100 percent in all that he does and is moving at a clip more impressive than ever while constructing his latest restaurant, Blue Fin. Currently Chang can boast of having Houston's premier restaurant destination, Uptown Sushi.

This chic site for sushi lovers opened its doors in late 2003. Since then the ritzy, raw fish hotspot has become a favorite of those with discriminating palates and it doesn't show signs of slowing down, much like its owner. Nearly every night in Uptown Park, discerning crowds arrive in droves, drawn in by the spectacular decor and inventive offerings of the freshest sushi and Japanese fusion cuisine.

The innovative architectural interior design entails vanilla silk curtains draped among camel-colored banquettes and Philippe Starck chairs that complement the brushed aluminum accents in a stadium-seating environment. With this elegant style, it's no accident that the swank locale has a feminine feel, making it the "It" place for the in-crowd. Chang says, "Over the past decade, women have rivaled men in the consumption of sushi. Because of this trend, I created a soft, feminine decor and atmosphere to draw women in. We all know where the women go, the men seem to follow." Once they're there, Chang likes to keep his patrons on their toes by changing the menu on a whim.

What to wear: Often compared with restaurants in New York or Miami, Uptown Sushi draws a trendy clientele who wants to see and be seen, and they dress accordingly.

Uptown Sushi
1131 Uptown Park Boulevard, Suite 14
Houston, TX 77056
713-871-1200

ABOVE Vincent's wood-fired rotisserie chicken is a Houston favorite.

RIGHT Grappino's, a sister restaurant to Vincent's, has a private wine room that is perfect for parties.

VINCENT'S RESTAURANT

Vincent and Mary Mandola, proprietors

"When a guest says to me, 'This feels like a piece of Italy,' that's what I want to hear," says Vincent Mandola, who for nearly 30 years has been serving hungry Houstonians some of the finest regional Italian dishes at four Mandola family restaurants.

Vincent's was the second to open, in 1984, after the astounding success of his first restaurant, Nino's. The menu is a solid selection of authentic and satisfying dishes like hearty pizzas, homemade focaccia, and aglio arrosto, hot from the wood-burning pizza oven. But savory spit-roasted lemon and garlic chicken from the wood-fired rotisserie is the house specialty; customers never seem to get enough.

So popular is the food at Vincent's that in February 2005, along with their daughters, Vinceanne and Dana, Vincent and his wife, Mary, launched their latest concept. Just a few blocks from the other Mandola properties, Pronto Cucinino, a fast-casual Italian eatery, offers the famous spit-roasted chicken and other great foods with quick in-and-out service for people on the go.

At all of their restaurants, family members are always on hand to welcome guests with a warm greeting and a smile that says, "We love what we do, and we're sure you're going to love it, too."

What to wear: Dressy casual.

Vincent's Restaurant
2701 West Dallas Street
Houston, TX 77019
713-528-4313
www.ninos-vincents.com

Brian Carabet

Brian is owner and president of Signature Publishing Group. His favorite restaurant is The French Room in Dallas. The memory of a seven course, four hour dinner with his beautiful wife made it the most awesome restaurant experience ever.

Danny Piassick

Danny's favorite restaurant is the Original Market Diner on Harry Hines Boulevard in Dallas. He frequents this place because it is so close to his studio and he craves the chicken fried steak.

Jolie Carpenter

Her favorite restaurant is The Gristmill in New Braunfels, her hometown. She's been eating there since she was 5 years old and it's a family favorite. The views from the decks, hovered in oak trees of the Guadalupe River are awesome!

Karla Setser

Most of my favorite places are in this book! I think the regional cuisine of Texas is unique. I enjoy the spice and fire of Mexican food in San Antonio, the eclectic Dallas dining scene and the comfort and laid-back atmospheres of restaurants of Houston and Austin.

Allison Hatfield

She is a New York-based writer and Texas expat. Her favorite restaurant is the tiny, charming Lola, located in Uptown Dallas. Unflaggingly romantic like Allison herself, Lola's fine food, wine and service make her heart sing.

Additional Acknowledgements

Project Management - Carol Kendall
Traffic Coordination - Elizabeth Gionta, Chris Nims, and Kristy Randall
Design - Mary Elizabeth Acree, Emily Kattan, and Mishelle Cunninham-Scott

Photography Credits

RIGHT Jolie, Chris and Mico at The Mercury Grill.

The Design Industries Foundation Fighting AIDS turned 20 in 2004. With 15 chapters and community partners, DIFFA is one of the largest funders of HIV/AIDS service and education programs in the United States. Since its founding in 1984, DIFFA has mobilized the immense resources of the design communities to provide more than $31 million to hundreds of AIDS organizations nationwide.

Started with volunteers from fashion, interior design and architecture, DIFFA now has supporters from every field associated with fine design. DIFFA's fundraising activities are among the most celebrated in AIDS philanthropy.

DIFFA grants are available to AIDS service organizations that provide preventative educational programs targeted at populations at risk of infection, treatment and direct-care services for people living with AIDS, and public policy initiatives that contribute resources to private sector efforts.

AIDS is not over. Find out how you can help DIFFA work toward a world without AIDS by visiting www.DIFFA.org.

DIFFA Dallas
1400 Turtle Creek Blvd., Suite 147
Dallas, Texas 75207
214-748-8580

DIFFA Houston
P.O. Box 131605
Houston, Texas 77219
713-528-0505